Free Enterprise Without Poverty

He who does not reward his cormorant
for catching fish will go hungry.

CHINESE PROVERB

Our government assumes that man,
unlike all other animals, is willing
to work without incentives.

L. M. G.

Leonard M. Greene

Free
Enterprise
Without
Poverty

W·W·NORTON & COMPANY
NEW YORK   LONDON

Published simultaneously in Canada by George J. McLeod Limited, Toronto.
Printed in the United States of America
All Rights Reserved
First Edition

Library of Congress Cataloging in Publication Data

Greene, Leonard M.
    Free enterprise without poverty.
    Includes index.
    1. Public welfare—United States. I. Title.
HV95.G69   1981   361.6'0973   81-2512
ISBN 0-393-01470-3   AACR2

W. W. Norton & Company, Inc. 500 Fifth Avenue, New York, N.Y. 10110
W. W. Norton & Company Ltd. 25 New Street Square, London EC4A 3NT

1 2 3 4 5 6 7 8 9 0

Contents

Foreword   11

Introduction

                                                                            15
Welfare and Free Enterprise: Two Systems
The Need for Reform

CHAPTER 1
Rich Uncle: Government Income Transfers   23
   Kinds of Income Support   25
   Income Support and Need   27
   Who Provides Income Support?   28
   State Programs   29
   "Don't Forget Me!"   29

CHAPTER 2
Categorical Aid: Welfare's Catch-22   31
   What's Wrong with Categorical Aid?   32
   The Major Programs   35
   Why There Is a Welfare Mess   37

CHAPTER 3
Why Work?   41
   The Welfare Tax   42
   The High Cost of Working   43

CHAPTER 4

Good-Bye Daddy   45
  Fostering a Divided Society   46
  The Growth of the Fatherless Family   47
  Destroying Families by Welfare Policy   49
  Setting Father Free: Relief from Support
    Payments   51

CHAPTER 5

Social Insecurity   53
  Social Security: Insurance or Welfare   54
  Disability Insurance: The Blank Check   59

CHAPTER 6

The Compensations of Unemployment   63
  The Private Sector: Promoting
    Dependency   69

CHAPTER 7

The War to End Welfare   72
  The War on Poverty   73
  Bureaucratic Problems   75
  The Growth of the Dependency System   79

CHAPTER 8

The Struggle to Reform Welfare   81

CHAPTER 9

Energy Aid: A New Example of Welfare
  Proliferation   89
  The Federal Programs   90
  Patchwork: The States Respond   94

CHAPTER 10

Solving the Welfare "Mess": The Graduated
  Income Supplement   106
  The Problems of Piecemeal Reform   107

Contents 9

The Need for Comprehensive Reform 110
The First Step: "Cashing Out" 112
Eligibility: Putting Everyone on the Same
  Footing 115
Does Supplementing Income Provide
  Work Incentives? 117
Toward a National Standard 118
The Role of the Tax System 119
The Economic Implications of the
  Graduated Income Supplement 121

CHAPTER 11

Paying the Piper 124
Putting a Lid on Welfare Spending:
  The Role of Substitution 125

CHAPTER 12

The First Step: A New Incremental Approach 128
Principles for an Incremental Approach 129
Introducing the Graduated Income
  Supplement by Increments 131

Summary 134

APPENDIX

An Analysis of a Taxable Demogrant 137
Tables and Figures 155

Index 187

Foreword

We as a nation have accumulated various welfare laws as if we were members of a lifeboat, with each of us voting for special rations. The benefit for each special interest group has been given preference over the benefit of all.

The question must therefore be faced: Do we possess the resources to fulfill these commitments, and is the social and political turmoil created by these divisions of resources sufficient to overturn the stability of our society?

The twofold purpose of this book is to identify how we have arrived at this dangerous point and to propose the creative solution which I believe a compassionate nation is capable of implementing.

Friends have asked why I, as a mathematician and the founder of a computer manufacturing corporation, devote so much time to the study of social welfare policy and macroeconomics. Why, for instance, have I established and over the years funded The Institute for Socioeconomic Studies?

One very self-serving aim is to attain something better than a favored position on a sinking ship. Our country cannot be strong and genuinely viable again until we solve the welfare mess.

My career in business has shown me the devastating effects that welfare has on people. I have gained firsthand knowledge of these effects by employing others—and by being employed by others. Some of the persons to whom I allude in this book have worked at the corporation which I head. Others include the good men and women I have encountered during recent years, when I have taken time off to work as an unskilled laborer—as a dishwasher, sledgehammer assembly man, caddy, and the like. These "demeaning" experiences created important friendships and memories for me.

We have all learned, at some point in our lives, that the government giveth and the government taketh away. This pattern gives rise to the social distortions to which both welfare recipients and taxpayers have been subject. The conclusion of this book is that welfare should be gradually phased out, while a Graduated Income Supplement should be phased in.

This book is written for the lay reader. Those who prefer a more technical analysis of the subject may be interested in the summary (included in the Appendix) of a project that laid the groundwork for many of my conclusions.

Under my direction, a team of researchers analyzed the fiscal implications of implementing a Graduated Income Supplement, in this project referred to as a taxable demogrant. Cost estimates were made assuming that the demogrant would substitute for existing benefits and would be taxable. I wish to thank the people who labored at length on this difficult task, namely Dr. Eli Sagi, Dr. James Albrecht, Gad Ariav, and Bette K. Fishbein.

In completing this book, I feel obliged to acknowledge and express special thanks for the consistently painstaking work that members of the staff of The Institute for Socioeconomic Studies—including B. A. Rittersporn, Jr., and Lloyd R. Targer—have given to research on which I based my program. Their work and the encouragement and support of my wife and children have helped make this volume possible.

LEONARD M. GREENE

White Plains, N.Y.
March 1981

Introduction

A few years ago, my company had an opening for a computer technician. Following our usual policy, we referred the notice of the vacancy to the New York State Employment Service. We had always found that when we hired people not often sought by other employers—victims of poverty, physical disability, or mandatory retirement—we ended up with highly motivated and dependable workers.

The personnel manager recommended that we hire a black teenager referred to us by the employment service. A high-school dropout from a poor family in the Bronx slums, he seemed bright and determined to find a career for himself.

By hiring him, we would take a significant risk. The job required six months of training in assembling and operating sophisticated instruments. If he failed anywhere along the way—always possible with any new worker—our investment would be lost and we would have to start all over again.

Fortunately, he worked out well. Although unfamiliar with the rigors of regular work in a plant, he learned quickly and displayed a positive attitude. Suddenly, just three months after he had started, he quit.

Before he left, I called him to my office. I wanted to know why he was leaving just when everything seemed to be going so well. Quietly and without trying to hide his disappointment, he told me a surprising story. His family lived in a crumbling building in the Bronx, perhaps one of the most devastated areas in urban America. Three years earlier, the family had applied for subsidized housing in a new development. Finally, word had come that they were eligible to move into a new apartment in the Park Ridge houses.

There was just one problem: the family could earn no more than a fixed amount of money to retain its eligibility. If its members earned more, they would have to stay in their slum dwelling until they could buy their way out. After all the years of waiting, the family could wait no longer. They decided that my young employee must quit his job so that they could live better.

In a couple of days, the youth picked up his last paycheck, and I never saw him again. Yet I often wonder what happened to him. With all of his obvious ambition, I'm sure that he is not idly staying at home. With his get-up-and-go, he may now be running numbers on the streets—or worse. I am certain that a good part of the current 38 percent unemployment among young blacks is due to this kind of work disincentive.

This incident continues to haunt me; the youth was a victim of a program that was intended to help him. The new apartment is in a project partially funded by federal money. The Department of Housing and Urban Development pays the building's owner the difference between what the tenants can provide and the rental rate on the open market. If a family is able to pay more than the predetermined amount because of an even slight increase in its income, it must be barred from the apartment. In an unusual way, the poor family is subject to a high income tax, far higher than middle-class people would tolerate. For them, an additional dollar of income can end up costing the family its home.

Welfare and Free Enterprise: Two Systems

The case of this young man was not unusual, I discovered. Time and again, people trying to climb out of poverty or to overcome disadvantages find themselves victims of the relentless "welfare system" that operates to perpetuate itself and, more important, results in the denial of hope to millions of people.

Fortunately, most of us never have to submit to this system. We are the beneficiaries of a free enterprise economy based on rewarding achievement. Usually, a worker's pay is based on his output. By providing incentives to work and to earn, our economic system insures increasing productivity. Of course, some people are better rewarded than others, because some people are more productive than others.

This free enterprise system has given the United States a level of economic development unsurpassed in the world. Best of all, it offers anybody a chance to share in the national prosperity.

Despite this economic opportunity, some people cannot participate—through no fault of their own. They cannot respond to the incentives of the system because they are involuntarily poor, uneducated, disabled, or old. For much of our history, assistance to these unfortunate people was left to private agencies. "The maintenance of the poor, which being merely a matter of charity, cannot be deemed expended in the administration of government," said Thomas Jefferson. The government which he had done so much to fashion adhered to his stand down through the years.

Not until the pervasive unemployment and poverty resulting from the Great Depression made the burden too heavy for private philanthropy and self-help did social welfare programs take root in the government. During the administration of Franklin D. Roosevelt government action was therefore greatly expanded—but only as a temporary departure from the Jeffersonian standard. Roosevelt himself ultimately acknowledged, "The lessons of history, confirmed by the evidence immediately before me, show conclusively that continued dependence upon relief induces a spiritual and moral disintegration fundamentally destructive to the national fiber. To dole out relief in this way is to administer a narcotic, a subtle destroyer of the human spirit."

President Roosevelt was right. The programs he began and their descendants have promoted dependency and sapped the human spirit.

Because many people on welfare would end up with less money if they took jobs, they refrain from making the effort to become self-supporting. In a country supposedly dominated by the "work ethic," we have created a "welfare system" that encourages people to go on "relief" and stay there.

In fact, what could reasonably be called the dependency system is actually harmful to free enterprise. Productivity is essential to economic growth, but the system discourages people who might well become productive workers from taking jobs. Some might argue, however, that there is already high unemployment. Doesn't welfare provide an income to those who cannot find jobs?

Such a question reflects a simplistic understanding of our current economic crisis. While unemployment is apparently too high, many jobs go begging. It is difficult to find apprentices to replace retired skilled workers. This "dependency system" removes any incentive for the poor to take relatively low-paying, entry-level jobs.

The Need for Reform

Eliminating the "dependency system" by developing a mechanism that takes care of the needs of the unemployable while providing incentives for those able to work could be the key to improving productivity. That would enable our economic system to deliver the benefits which it is capable of delivering.

Just about everyone agrees that welfare must be reformed. Three presidents—Nixon, Ford, and Carter—have proposed comprehensive plans for reform only to see them defeated by Congress. Lack of understanding and preoccupation with the enormous cost have combined to block basic reform.

Our past efforts at reform have bred cynicism and pessimism. Perhaps the main reason for our failure has been our unwillingness to recognize that the basic cause of the inefficacy of our current approach is its failure to provide a reasonable incentive to work.

If we place welfare in its proper setting, among all of the government programs providing income support, we may be able to arrive at a broad reform that will make our economic system more efficient.

No needy person should be deprived of the public assistance that virtually everyone deems fair and reasonable.

Nor should any person capable of work be prevented from finding a job because of the tempting disincentives of public assistance.

America must find a way to combine its pledge that no

one need live in poverty with its promise that the benefits of productive labor shall flow to those who work. Somehow, we have lost sight of the connection between these two principles. The welfare underclass has been allowed to develop alongside the free enterprise system. If we will lift our eyes from today's welfare mess and the problems of seemingly perennial inflation and unemployment to a future order in which our economic system can function properly, we have a chance to bring about the necessary reform.

Free
Enterprise
Without
Poverty

CHAPTER 1

Rich Uncle

Government Income Transfers

Recently, a group of angry fishermen in Portland, Maine, met with federal government officials. A few years earlier, the fishermen had demanded that the United States claim a 200-mile limit in order to prevent foreign fishing interests from overfishing American waters. The government had met the earlier demand. Now the meeting was called to review the success of the new fishing limit.

The only problem was that the new limit was not a success. The law establishing the 200-mile limit gave the government the right to set quotas so that the North Atlantic would not be fished out. As a result, New England fishermen found they were spending a lot of time in port because they could easily fill their quotas in just a few days. In fact, the new quotas were so small, they maintained, that they could no longer even make the payments on their boats.

Moreover, it turned out that the fishermen wanted their own form of welfare. If the government refused to increase the quotas, the fishermen said, they wanted federal payments to make up for their lost income. They argued that as farmers have been paid to keep land out of cultivation, so they should be paid not to fish. The federal government currently has various kinds of aid programs for growers of tobacco, sugar, cotton, wheat, feed grain, and rice, for sheep and dairy farmers, and for beekeepers.

A recent study, done under the auspices of The Institute for Socioeconomic Studies, attempted to identify all such federally sponsored programs, including both programs clearly identified as income support and those which have that effect, even though they may have been designed for another purpose. It revealed that, in the fiscal year 1977, there were 182 federal income-support programs, involving an annual cost of $248 billion. For each dollar of federal tax receipts that year, about sixty-nine cents were spent in direct or indirect income support.

A second study was conducted, covering state and local expenditures on income support. It revealed that, in fiscal 1977, these levels of government spent about $50 billion on such programs.

The magnitude of these expenditures makes clear that very few Americans are not eligible for some kind of government income-support program. The variety of such programs testifies to the unstinting effort made by policymakers to "be responsive" to the economic needs and political pressures of hundreds of groups within our society.

Almost a third of these programs are small, by government standards, involving expenditures of less than $50 million a year, but one-fifth of the programs have annual budgets of $1 billion or more. The five major elements of the national Social Security system—retirement, survivors' and disability pensions, Medicare hospital and medical payments—account for two out of every five dollars spent for income support.

Kinds of Income Support

Federal income support is provided in the form of cash, in-kind assistance, tax relief and credit, or insurance.

We can easily recognize some of the programs providing cash assistance. Aid to Families with Dependent Children (AFDC) is the major element of welfare; it provided some $5.7 billion in cash benefits in fiscal 1977. Social Security retirement insurance, by which $52.4 billion was transferred from taxpayers to retirees, is undoubtedly the largest cash program.

But the wool and mohair payment program of the Department of Agriculture may not be so familiar. If you own sheep or lambs and sell their wool or the unshorn lambs, you may be eligible for benefits. Similarly, if you own Angora goats and sell mohair, you may also be in line for payments based on the difference between the average market price you would receive and the higher, government-support price. The government makes direct cash payments, and you are free to spend the money any way you wish. This program is a modest one, costing just $8 million. Nonetheless, it is just as much an income-support program as is Social Security.

A substantial amount of assistance takes the form of in-kind aid. Under these programs, recipients are provided with goods and services, paid for by the government, rather than with cash. Medicare hospital and supplementary medical benefits account for two-fifths of all in-kind aid. But there are a great number of other medical programs, many intended for veterans, which also involve in-kind aid.

Other in-kind assistance programs provide food and nutritional assistance, housing, educational training, and social services. Among these programs are the $1.1 billion effort to provide low-income housing, the $115 million spent to provide preschool children with free or reduced-price meals, the $245 million which goes for direct health-care services for American Indians and Alaskan natives, and the $7.8 billion Food Stamp program.

According to The Institute's *Inventory of Federal Income Transfer Programs,* in 1977 some $35 billion in support was provided through tax relief. Increasingly, economists have come to regard preferences provided in the tax laws as a form of government spending—the tax expenditure. These preferences are always designed to benefit specific groups, and they amount to a form of income supplementation. The decision to provide such exemptions deprives the government of revenues it would otherwise receive. Under the relatively new congressional budget process, new tax preferences are measured in terms of the impact on governmental receipts.

There are no fewer than twenty-eight exemptions, deductions, exclusions, and credits in the Internal Revenue Code which provide some form of income support. The largest, in terms of dollars, is the right of employers to exclude from taxable income the contributions they make to pension plans for their employees. In effect, employers can provide retirement coverage at a reduced cost, because they are not required to use after-tax dollars. Government becomes a partner in paying for pensions at an annual cost of $8.7 billion.

One of the smallest of the tax programs has been the exclusion from income of the capital gain realized by the taxpayers over sixty-five when they sell their homes. In 1977 this exclusion cost only $40 million. However, as is so often the case, a small program is on the way to becoming a big one. In 1978 Congress decided to expand the exemp-

tion and to lower the age of eligibility to fifty-five. Undoubtedly, the cost will increase substantially, and it is reasonable
to expect that, in later years, the program will be further
expanded.

Finally, income support may take the form of credit or
insurance. One of these programs is veterans' life insurance, which is funded by appropriations as well as by
premiums. The small Indian Credit program, under which
low-interest loans, loan guarantees, and insurance are
made available to Indians and Alaskan natives for economic
development on reservations, is a further example.

Income Support and Need

Income-support programs can be viewed from another
perspective. It might be assumed that many, if not most, of
these programs were created to provide financial assistance
to those in need. Yet the majority of these programs are not
conditioned on need.

The AFDC program (our stereotype of "welfare") is,
of course, directly related to the income and wealth of
recipients. The exclusion of sick pay by the disabled from
their taxable income is a program that is partly determined
by need. Many programs for older people are not directly
conditioned on need, but have some characteristics of a
need-related program, simply because most older people
live on reduced incomes. Finally, some benefits, ranging
from the tax exclusion for the sale of a home for those over
fifty-five to flood insurance, are provided if beneficiaries
meet certain requirements, but their income level is not
one of these.

Who Provides Income Support?

A final way to look at federal income-support programs is in terms of the agencies that administer them. Some 55 percent of them are under the control of the Department of Health, Education, and Welfare (HEW).

Interestingly, the Department of Agriculture is a major welfare agency, handling the massive Food Stamp program and other, smaller in-kind nutrition programs for the needy. These programs were originally conceived as aiding farmers in the disposal of surplus crops, but they remained under the aegis of the Agriculture Department long after their purpose shifted to welfare.

The Internal Revenue Service is yet another "welfare" agency, because of the twenty-four tax preferences which it handles and which result in income support. Obviously, all of these benefits are in cash.

Another major area is veterans' benefits, almost all of which are handled by the Veterans Administration. Principal programs include compensation for service-connected disabilities, education assistance, and hospitals. In addition, the Defense Department manages the massive military retirement program.

Although these agencies account for the greatest part of federal income support, a dozen others also have significant programs. Each agency is presumably able to meet the specific needs of its own constituency. For example, there are eleven distinct programs relating to veterans' health care. On the other hand, the cost of maintaining so many agencies that are in the business of providing income support is high. But this decentralization and multiplication of benefits breeds confusion, too. Simply by not going to the correct office, an eligible person may miss out on benefits.

State Programs

The bewildering complexity of federal income transfers is compounded by the income-support programs of the states. Although it might appear at first glance that many changes at the federal level would leave the plethora of state programs intact, on closer examination it is evident that the states and localities actually spend relatively little money on income support in programs not directly influenced by Washington. Of the $50 billion spent by state and local governments, almost two-thirds were triggered directly or indirectly by federal programs.

"Don't Forget Me!"

A review of this kaleidoscope of benefit programs brings out the urgent need to systematize and *simplify* our efforts to provide income assistance. But pressure to add more and more programs is unrelenting. Remember the New England fishermen whom I mentioned earlier. They demand their own program, loudly citing the income support provided to farmers. After the fishermen, who next will insist on being aided? Will that group really be aware of—or care about—the burden heaped upon our country by any effort to fashion special programs for special needs?

Perhaps those who want more of the same should talk to a man I met, the former owner of a small family farm in Iowa. He told me that he never had enough acreage to spare in order to take advantage of government programs which would pay him to keep some of his land out of cultivation. Almost all of his farm was devoted to producing fodder for his livestock and food for his family. He sold some of his produce in the local market, but his operation was not big enough for him to qualify for government crop-support programs. What he needed was cash to keep his family going. He could find some cash in the marketplace. But it was not enough, and the government provided no real supplementary help. Finally, he sold the farm and moved into town. He and his children took jobs in the factory. They joined the thirty million people who have left rural America for the cities since the beginning of World War II.

Many would say that his departure from the farm was inevitable, given the growing strength of large-scale, corporate agriculture. Perhaps that is true, but it evades the issue: the federal government created programs supposedly designed to help this man keep his farm. These programs may have contributed to the growth of large farms and to corporate agriculture. They provided the wrong kind of aid: many small farmers did not need price support; they needed income support.

The most obvious conclusion from our survey of income-support programs is that, whatever they were called, they were intended basically to assure recipients of a certain level of income. But they have often resulted in something else, and when they have, people like the Iowa farmer may have ended up empty-handed.

CHAPTER 2

Categorical Aid
Welfare's Catch-22

A young girl in New York City contracted an unusual and incurable illness. The muscles of her throat were paralyzed. She could not speak and could subsist only on a special liquid diet. In the hope that she could learn to take care of herself, she was sent to a children's hospital for rehabilitative training. After having undergone successful treatment, she was told that she could return home.

No course of continuing treatment was needed. Her only special requirement was liquid food costing $4 a day. It is at that point that things got stuck. There was no program under which she could obtain government payments to cover her daily costs of $4. Her mother was receiving Social Security survivors' benefits. The addition of the $4 a day would make the family's income too high to allow the girl to collect her daily allotment. The only "solution" was for the daughter to remain in the hospital! So she remained there. The government spent $135 a day under the Medicaid program for $4 worth of food.

This story demonstrates just one effect of the intricacies of diverse income-support plans, each with its own eligibility rules. Such programs, especially those directly associated with welfare, are specifically designed for people who meet precisely defined sets of characteristics. To a great extent, these categorical classifications were born out of a desire to limit waste and cheating. The rules and regulations try to do so by clearly identifying eligible participants in each program.

What's Wrong with Categorical Aid?

People don't easily fit into categories. Even a description like "disabled" often defies simple classification. In 1978 there were 2.2 million people receiving federal SSI payments for the disabled. The SSI rolls contain many people with arguable disabilities. Distinguishing mental and emotional difficulties is a particular problem. Sadly, however, others who are truly unemployable and needy fail to qualify.

The categorization of people also promotes socially disruptive behavior. AFDC benefits are generally intended for single-parent families. This has prompted thousands of fathers to leave home so that the children qualified for government aid. Indeed, we now begin to perceive that when assistance is granted only to those in certain categories, people will alter their circumstances in order to fit into the categories—or at least pretend to alter them.

People are frequently eligible for help under more than one program. A 1976 study by the Rand Corporation showed that an average New York City welfare family benefited from seven different programs. Yet, as with the seventeen-year-old New York girl, the requirements of one program can conflict directly with those of another. And, as in that case, the attempt to reduce waste in welfare programs by the use of the categorical programs can actually result in even greater waste.

In the New York case, the conflict between two programs was clear. The Social Security benefits received by the family were not conditioned on need, so they would be paid no matter what other income the family had. At the same time, the health benefits for in-home care were related to need, and the Social Security payments themselves provided the family too much money for it to qualify.

This kind of conflict can manifest itself in a number of different ways. A few years ago, a New York fire chief actually demoted himself when he discovered that he could get greater medical benefits if he took a lower rank and lower pay. His wife was seriously ill and needed to be hospitalized. The cost of her medical care was greater than the amount of money the man would lose by dropping down in rank. The net effect of the medical plan's eligibility rules was thus to cause the loss of the fire chief's services. And the man himself must have suffered because he was deprived of the opportunity to employ his talents to the fullest.

The use of categorical programs can also result in people's receiving more gross income than was intended. According to one congressional study, a woman with three children in a large southern city was receiving $422 a month in earnings, $81 in AFDC, $59 in public-housing aid, $16 worth of surplus commodities, $38 in child care, $14 worth of assistance through the school-lunch program, and $48 in Medicaid payments—a total of $678 in monthly benefits. A working woman who was receiving no benefits would have had to earn more than $800 a month to obtain the same after-tax income. At the time of the study, the average monthly wage for women was actually $500 a month. The woman in the study was thus receiving a respectable income by combining her eligibility for several programs, and she had no incentive to seek work.

Welfare critics have frequently criticized recipients for combining welfare benefits in this way, but it is not really their fault. Who can argue with their desire to get the most money they can for their families.

Yet combining benefits from several programs can prove to be a destructive force in the lives of the recipients. In one instance, a woman gave up trying to find a job when she realized that she could never earn enough to make it worthwhile for her to look for work—rather than to continue to accept welfare. Now forty years old, the woman has been receiving welfare benefits most of her life. Born to parents on welfare, she recently saw her own daughter go on the welfare rolls. The three children of her daughter have become the fourth generation in the family to be supported by welfare payments. In fact, there is now a permanent welfare "class" of millions of people.

Because of quirks in the laws governing the various welfare programs, so-called notches can develop in the benefit eligibility rules. A notch occurs when the rules require benefits to end if the recipient earns more than a specified amount. The phasing out of benefits is not gradual; it is abrupt. The result is a large loss in total income if earned income exceeds the notch even by one dollar.

A fifty-six-year-old Minnesota man was receiving Social Security benefits when the government informed him that they would be increased by fourteen dollars a month. He could not refuse to accept the increase, unless he dropped out of the program entirely. But that small increase meant that he automatically lost his eligibility for Medicaid. There was no gradual reduction in the Medicaid benefits for which he was eligible; he lost them all when his income went up slightly. In addition, the price of his food stamps went up, as did the cost of his subsidized housing, and his veterans' pension was reduced. In the end he lost far more than fourteen dollars—all because there was no coordination among government programs.

The Major Programs

Programs to aid the poor fall into one of three classifications: social insurance, income support, and job creation.

Social-insurance programs provide assistance to people, most of whom have contributed to the financing and who meet certain eligibility criteria not related to their financial need. The largest of these programs in the basic Social Security system, officially called Old Age, Survivors, and Disability Insurance. Originally conceived as a form of insurance, this program was not intended to provide benefits according to need. Instead, working people were to contribute to it and later receive benefits conditioned on their contributions. The rich as well as the poor were to be eligible for payments. Social Security was not really meant to be a form of insurance, under which a person's contributions would be invested and used later to pay his or her benefits. In fact, today's workers contribute to the benefits paid to today's recipients, and they must expect that tomorrow's workers will take care of them. Over the years, the program has been continually expanded.

Unemployment compensation is yet another such program. An Unemployment Trust Fund is fed by money from federal and state taxes on employers' payrolls. Actually these "contributions" are payroll deductions from employees, who, in the absence of the program, might expect to receive the amount of the taxes in their paychecks. In the fiscal year 1977 there were about ten million beneficiaries.

Medicare is a relatively recent addition to the social-insurance spectrum. A supplementary medical-insurance program which pays some nonhospital expenses is supported by premiums. In 1976 over twenty-four million people were involved in these programs.

The most well-known program is Aid to Families with Dependent Children (AFDC). The intention of the program is to insure that children in families where there is little or no earned income are guaranteed a minimal budget for survival. Under AFDC, cash aid is usually given to families headed by a woman, on the theory that she must stay at home to take care of the children and thus cannot be expected to work. In 1976 over four million families participated. A great many of them were also covered by other welfare programs.

Supplemental Security Income (SSI), a part of Social Security, goes to blind and disabled people and to those sixty-five and older if their incomes fall below a level set nationally. Over four million people were receiving monthly payments in 1977; about half of them were aged.

Food stamps are provided by the federal government to people who meet certain income and eligibility standards. The stamps may be used instead of cash in making food purchases. This program is designed to help not only the poor, but also the farmers, who gain additional outlets for their products through its operations. In 1977 over seven million households received food stamps.

Other nutritional programs are aimed at children, and they provide what amounts to an indirect subsidy to both the poor and the nonpoor. The best known of these are the school-lunch and the school-breakfast programs.

Medicaid is a massive health-care financing program for welfare recipients and other poor people. Medicaid has grown rapidly, and more than twenty-four million people receive care under it each year.

Among the other major benefit programs are housing assistance, basic-education-opportunity grants, social-service grants, and veterans' pensions. For poor people who encounter unusual financial difficulties in a given month, many states provide "emergency assistance." Some states also give "general assistance" to those needy people who do not qualify for federal cash aid programs.

Still another benefit for the poor is the Earned Income Tax Credit. It reduces the taxes of those who earn low wages. In cases in which a family's taxes are less than the credit, the surplus is refunded to the family in cash.

Some employment programs are targeted especially at the poor. CETA, the Comprehensive Employment and Training Act, provides public service jobs. The work-incentive (WIN) program has been used to provide training and job-placement services to those on welfare, and it gives employers a tax incentive to hire the poor. Hundreds of thousands of people are employed under these programs.

Why There Is a Welfare Mess

These are merely the largest and best known of the programs that are commonly called welfare. They are indeed enormous, as is the bureaucracy that must administer them. In 1977 the cost of administering AFDC, Medicaid, CETA, and Food Stamps was at least $1.8 billion, and probably a great deal more. These funds went to hire hundreds of thousands of people on the federal, state, and local levels to help people determine their eligibility, to insure that they got their proper benefits, and to check on cheats. We actually spent more on administering a handful of welfare programs than on community health centers, the development of health maintenance organizations, maternal and child health services, Head Start, nutrition programs for the elderly, and the like.

This expenditure on welfare bureaucracy is more than just a tremendous waste: it leads to massive confusion. Substantial resources may be allocated to determining whether people are eligible for certain programs, only to have them go through an entirely different eligibility screening for other programs.

The categorical approach is, in turn, an open invitation to cheating. Potential beneficiaries can slip between the cracks, simply because there are so many cracks. In addition to outright fraud, the complexity of the system results in a substantial number of errors. Some fraud and error can be eliminated if the federal government gives the states and localities financial incentives to reduce them. But the sheer size of the various programs, and their often overlapping eligibility rules, guarantees that it will be impossible to eliminate these abuses entirely. In the Medicaid program alone, overpayments due to fraud and error amount to $1.5 billion a year.

The many welfare programs tend to spawn their own constituencies. Once a new class of beneficiaries is established, so is a new interest group which will use all of its political resources to maintain and strengthen its benefits. This situation favors strongly the addition of new programs and enhances the momentum toward an even more serious welfare mess.

The complexity of the system as a result of the categorical approach is increased by the existence of myriad state programs intended to supplement those on the federal level. The Institute for Socioeconomic Studies conducted an inventory of state and local income-transfer programs which showed that the twenty-five largest states had 633 programs of their own. The heaviest financial burden falls on the states with the largest welfare populations. Almost inevitably, the size of its welfare population is a good indication of the economic problems facing a given state.

The differentials in welfare benefits among the states are enormous. In 1978 federal and state AFDC payments ranged from a low of 13.1 percent of the poverty level in Mississippi to a high of 108.4 percent in Hawaii.

Finally, the categorical approach means that the implementation of welfare policy is highly decentralized. Welfare lacks central control. What's more, welfare cannot easily respond to changes in national policy or in prevailing economic conditions. In fact, so long as the categorical approach is used, it will be almost impossible to alter national welfare policy. In order to reduce some welfare spending and to integrate welfare policy with other elements of economic policy, the categorical approach will necessarily have to be abandoned. In light of the abuses and the weakness of the prevailing system, the case against the current approach is strong.

The categorical programs provide that all those meeting the eligibility rules are entitled to aid. These "entitlements" now constitute 48 percent of the entire federal budget. Congress cannot reduce these costs without first changing the programs. The current $300-billion price tag will inexorably go up.

One crippled man found out just how these inequities of categorical aid can hurt. He had received a check for $2,275 which represented retroactive SSI payments for which he had been eligible, but for which he had not been paid. Although he continued to meet eligibility rules, this payment put him over the $1,500 limit on personal assets. As a result, he was out of the SSI program. Only later did authorities advise him that if he had spent his windfall promptly instead of letting it become part of his meager holdings, he would have remained eligible for aid. As long as categorical aid survives, such tragic cases will constitute a kind of continuing welfare Catch-22.

CHAPTER 3

Why Work?

Suppose that you were offered a promotion to a new position in your company. Of course, the job would entail greater responsibilities, and you would have to work harder and put in longer hours. Chances are that you would be glad to get the promotion.

But suppose your boss told you that if you took the new job, your salary would be cut by 30 percent and the company would no longer contribute to your medical insurance premiums. What's more, you would have to begin paying for the parking space and cafeteria lunch that the company had provided you free of charge until now. You might then be a lot less enthusiastic about the new job. In fact, you might turn down the opportunity to gain greater responsibility.

You have probably never heard of such a situation in actuality. It goes counter to common sense to promote somebody, give the person more work, and then cut his or her pay.

Yet welfare recipients who have the chance to take private-sector jobs face precisely that situation. The system for paying benefits is structured to penalize a person who is willing to leave welfare to take a job, perhaps quite low paying, that offers the hope of rising out of poverty. Despite the diversity of its defects, there is no question about the most serious weakness of the current welfare system: it operates to discourage work. In this way, the welfare system contains the seeds of its own failure. Whatever the will of the people and their elected officials, the system itself makes it impossible to realize Franklin D. Roosevelt's objective of gradually phasing out large-scale public assistance in favor of increased employment.

The antiwork bias built into the welfare system was the result of a policy based on the best of intentions. When Roosevelt's New Deal began to establish assistance programs for the poor, some criteria had to be chosen for determining who would be eligible for help. The most obvious way to distribute "relief" had always been to give it to those in need, to people lacking both the income and the assets to survive without help. Such an approach was not only compassionate; it was also practical. Assistance could be made available to those who required it most, and denied to those who did not demonstrate sufficient need.

The Welfare Tax

Although most people have never heard of it, the mechanism called the benefit reduction rate is at the heart of the welfare problem. This rate—or more properly these rates, because each public-assistance program has its own —is used to deal with the problem of reducing or taxing cash benefits as earnings increase. The purpose of the welfare tax is to deny benefits to those employed persons who do not need them. An undesirable by-product of this policy is work disincentive.

In practice it is extremely difficult to select the appropriate benefit reduction rate. If cash benefits are reduced by one dollar for every dollar that is earned—a benefit reduction rate of 100 percent—there will be absolutely no incentive for a person to take a job instead of staying on welfare. Or, at least, there will be no cash incentive.

Some maintain, however, that people would rather work than receive public assistance because of nomonetary incentives. For example, Gov. Hugh L. Carey of New York once told a congressional committee that "in the real world, the marginal economics of 'low benefit reduction rates' is not what makes people work. When decent jobs at decent wages are available, most welfare recipients, out of pride and self-respect, will take them eagerly."

But is what Governor Carey said altogether realistic? Think for a moment whether you would be willing to take that offered promotion if it meant substantial sacrifices in pay and benefits.

If the benefit reduction rate is lowered only slightly from 100 percent, in the belief that only a slight stimulus is needed to get people to shift from welfare to work, the incentive may not turn out to be meaningful. The new worker may have to pay travel and clothing expenses not incurred when on welfare. The apparent gain from taking the job may turn out to be a net loss.

The High Cost of Working

In the face of these numbers, you might expect that, even under the present welfare system, we would not have excessively high benefit reduction rates. You might reasonably count on our policy makers not to stifle all incentive to work, despite their desire not to pay benefits to people with earnings substantially above the poverty level. Well, you would be wrong. The actual "tax" rate of the AFDC program is 67 percent. A person earning $3.25 per hour actually gains only $1.07 when lost benefits are taken into account.

CHAPTER 4

Good-Bye Daddy

"We go to a young girl—a child of eighteen, or sixteen, or even younger—and this is what we say: Abandon all your hopes. Your schools will not teach you. You will not learn to read or write. You will never have a decent job. You will live in neighborhoods of endless unemployment and poverty, of drugs and violence.

"And then we say to this child: Wait, there is a way, one way, you can be somebody to someone. We will give you an apartment and furniture to fill it. We will give you a TV set and a telephone. We will give you clothing and cheap food and free medical care, and some spending money besides. And in return, you only have to do one thing: just go out there and have a baby. And faced with such an offer, it is no surprise that hundreds of thousands have been caught in the trap that our welfare system has become."

With these words, Sen. Edward M. Kennedy described what he called "the cancer of the soul which poisons the society." He might just as well have entitled his story "The Creation of a Welfare Mother," for just as surely as the welfare system provides incentives for people not to work, it also tempts them to break up their families or never to form them, thus destroying one of the important social units in our society. We see the social consequences of this breakdown all around us.

Fostering a Divided Society

Although we have a great many economic programs whose major impact falls on the family, and although we are supposedly dedicated to strengthening the family, any person familiar with our national policies quickly recognizes that we have no policy concerning the family and no plan for trying to maintain it as a functioning unit. While other countries have taken great pains to define policies specifically designed to benefit the family, the United States has acted as if it were of no importance. Every other Western industrial nation has a system of children's allowances that serves to assure the well-being of all its youth. Our country, unfortunately, has had since the 1930s a system that has often been destructive of families.

Nowhere is our indifference to the family, at least in terms of policy, more evident than in Aid to Families with Dependent Children. A policy that seemed to have reasonable underpinnings has turned out to have disastrous effects. At the outset, welfare policy showed special concern for children. They could not be blamed for their families' financial straits. Society had to make sure that they, as innocent victims, would be provided with at least a minimal standard of living. The most obvious reason for their poverty was the absence of one parent, almost always the father, from the home. The remaining parent, usually the mother, found it necessary to stay at home to care for them. This was understood to mean that no income was being earned to provide for their support.

Enter AFDC. It would provide assistance to lone mothers, to be used on behalf of the children. For the young woman, like the one Kennedy described, there would be a strong incentive not only to remain single, but to have a child. A similar incentive would encourage couples to break up their marriages. In either case, AFDC would destroy the family structure of America's poor.

Federal law has worked the other way around for nonpoor families. It tends to be helpful to them. For instance, the Internal Revenue Code provides a tax exemption of one thousand dollars for every child in a family. For the high-income taxpayer in the 50 percent bracket, this feature of the tax law can provide actual cash in hand of five hundred dollars. Without the exemption, that money would go to the tax collector. However, this provision does nothing to assist a poor family. It owes nothing to the tax collector to begin with and gets nothing from the exemption.

The Growth of the Fatherless Family

When AFDC was inaugurated in 1936, the absent father was the main factor in determining eligibility for the program. He still is, but the reasons for his absence have changed over the years. At the outset, a significant number of the fathers were absent because they were dead or incapacitated. In recent years, the largest share of AFDC cases has resulted simply from the physical absence of the father who was both alive and well. A study a few years ago showed that more than three-quarters of the AFDC case load resulted from simple absence. It is evident that the system promotes family dissolution all too effectively. It makes a split-up financially advantageous. The father as an individual is able to seek work, and the mother is left with the children and the welfare benefits. Close analysis reveals that in many cases of supposed breakup, the father and mother still have close, if clandestine, contact.

It is not surprising that the number of fatherless families has gone up rapidly since the end of World War II. At first, the cause was divorce and separation. Later, during the 1950s, the reasons could be found in the persistent recessions that plagued the economy, making it hard for the less skilled to find jobs, and apparently causing more family breakups.

Be that as it may, a major increase in AFDC participants took place in the first half of the 1960s, when the economy was expanding. The AFDC rolls grew from 3 million in 1960 to over 9.6 million in 1970. Nobody knows exactly why this happened. There were jobs. The divorce rate was not increasing. Moreover, other benefit programs were beginning to increase their coverage of children. Although positive proof may be lacking, it could reasonably be argued that, during this period, the incentive for family breakup—or, at least, for apparent family breakup—began to be a powerful force. In the latter part of the 1960s the trend continued and was just as puzzling to the experts. Yet it was noticed that those who had been the offspring of the postwar baby boom had now reached the age at which they would be parents. So the incentive for the fatherless family might well have been working at the same rate, but now with a larger number of people. At the same time, awareness of benefits under AFDC was growing rapidly, and welfare agencies became better equipped to encourage the poor to take advantage of those benefits.

By 1978 there were over 10.3 million people receiving AFDC benefits, at a cost of almost $11 billion.

As Senator Kennedy suggests, one consequence of the

AFDC rules has been to encourage women to seek public assistance through the relatively simple expedient of having a child. Faced with a society that seems unready to help them to become productive citizens, some women must find this path to welfare tempting. Although no authoritative statistics exist, it appears likely that many women choosing this course of action are themselves the children of welfare who have come to regard the welfare economy as the only one in which they can function. With an almost absolute certainty, we can expect the newborn to become one day candidates for the same process.

Destroying Families by Welfare Policy

AFDC not only fosters the creation of fatherless families, it encourages intact families to split. If a father deserted his family, the mother and children would be entitled to AFDC payments, food stamps, and Medicaid benefits. What if he deserted only to trigger this result and continued to work and to contribute to the support of the family? The incentive to dissolve the family bond or to cheat and make it seem that he deserted the family is almost overwhelming.

According to the director of the federal Office of Management and Budget, David A. Stockman, "the idea that adult couples would maintain an informal and episodic living arrangement in order to gain $5,000 in income undoubtedly offends our middle class values." Nonetheless, as Mr. Stockman argued as a congressman before joining President Reagan's cabinet, "any caseworker can attest to the fact that this practice is pervasive among the welfare population."

Some halfhearted efforts have been made to deal with

the problems arising from the so-called father-in-the-house rule. In the 1960s AFDC laws were changed to allow for some benefits for families in which the father was unemployed, but willing and able to work. Each state was given the option of permitting benefits under such circumstances. Disappointingly, only twenty-six decided to apply. Even where the AFDC-Unemployed Father option (allowing benefits to families with an unemployed breadwinner) is permitted, complicated eligibility rules make it impossible for many families to qualify. In May 1979 only 117,000 families nationwide benefited from this program.

In 1975 Congress enacted the Earned Income Tax Credit to provide some assistance to families in which the breadwinner was employed, without producing any incentive to breakup. Under its provisions, the working poor are entitled to a tax credit of 10 percent of the first $5,000 of earned income. As a result, the maximum benefit is $500. Once earned income goes past $5,000, the credit begins to be reduced. But, it may be argued, the full amount of the benefit available, the incentive to keep the family intact, is relatively small. And the Earned Income Tax Credit is obviously of no significance at all to a family with no earned income. Its impact in terms of the federal budget is small, too—amounting to less than $2 billion in the fiscal year 1981.

Although AFDC is most well-known for its destructive impact on family stability, almost all welfare programs have a similar effect. Income ceilings on eligibility for assistance invariably provide an incentive for families to break up and to divide, in fact or in appearance, the actual family revenues. Each part of the family attempts to keep its income below the cut-off line.

Perhaps the most extensive program which has this effect is Medicaid. In most states, AFDC recipients are au-

tomatically eligible for these benefits if they can demonstrate low family-income levels. A New York family of four
is considered "medically indigent" if its income is $5,000
or less. Because of the high cost of medical care, families
faced with big bills find that the incentive to break up in
order to keep income below the eligibility cut-off is a strong
one.

The case of an Indiana mother illustrates the high
social cost of the Medicaid eligibility rules. Stricken with
multiple sclerosis, she had to enter a nursing home to receive twenty-four-hour-a-day care. Without such attention,
she could not survive. Her husband, a meterman for a
power company, did not have medical insurance that covered nursing-home care. Even his entire annual salary of
$13,000 would not have been enough to pay the bills.

The family turned to Medicaid. The husband was told
that he would have to turn over to the state all but $400 of
his monthly income in order for his wife to qualify for
Medicaid. Yet the father and his three children could not
live on that amount. Faced with an impossible situation, the
couple made a heartbreaking decision to end their mar-
riage of sixteen years. The family could continue to live on
his income. The woman, lacking any income of her own,
would be eligible for complete Medicaid coverage of her
nursing-home bills.

Setting Father Free: Relief from Support Payments

When families break up, not because of the welfare
incentive, but because of incompatibility, the welfare system discourages the mother from trying to obtain support
payments from the father. In every state, child-support laws
require that parents accept the responsibility for assuring

their children of adequate financial support. Merely because the breadwinner leaves home does not relieve him of the obligation to provide that support. Child-support laws depend heavily on the parent left with custody of the children to file a complaint if payments are not made.

But the welfare system eliminates the incentive for the parent with custody, almost always the mother, to take action. The tax rate in terms of lost benefits is 100 percent when it comes to child-support payments. If the father does his duty toward his children, the family's AFDC benefits are reduced by one dollar for every dollar of support.

A 1973 study by the Department of Health, Education, and Welfare found that 83 percent of the fathers who were absent from the welfare household or who did not provide support actually had some ability to provide child support.

In short, the welfare system has become the great destroyer. Divorce and family breakup in order simply to obtain welfare benefits has become an accepted and largely unquestioned way of life. We have seen the development of a mentality that is willing to sacrifice family stability on the altar of benefits programs spread through our society.

Nursing homes may require elderly people who seek to enter to turn over their assets. As a result, welfare officials actually advise elderly couples to divorce. The partner remaining outside the home is to receive all of the assets. The other partner is ruled to be destitute and becomes eligible immediately for a wide variety of government programs.

CHAPTER 5

Social Insecurity

A sixty-eight-year-old retired accountant in New York City was offered $500 a month to use his skills to help a new business set up its books. Eager to keep up his skills, he gave serious consideration to the job offer. Then he began to calculate the real cost of going back to work. He realized that $84 would be deducted each month from his Social Security check because of his earnings. In addition, he would lose his eligibility for a local program that controlled rent increases in his apartment as well as for the reduced-rate fares he received on the mass-transit system. Unlike his government benefits, his earned income would be subject to income taxes, and he would also have to bear the burden of work-related expenses such as transportation and clothing. His bottom-line judgment was that it was simply not worth the financial sacrifice for him to return to work.

In short, welfare is not the only government assistance program which discourages people from taking jobs!

Social Security: Insurance or Welfare?

When Social Security was enacted in 1935, it was sold as an insurance program. Workers would purchase benefits through their contributions.

In fact, even the money paid on behalf of a worker by his or her employer is actually a contribution by the employee. But what the employee gets as wages, *plus* his employer's Social Security contributions, represents that employee's market value. What the employer has paid for the employee's Social Security actually constitutes forgone wages.

As insurance, Social Security would be expected to provide retirement payments, on the basis of contributions, no matter what the economic status of the retiree. Nevertheless, even at the outset, Social Security provided for a loss of benefits if the recipient's earnings went too high. Paul H. Douglas, a nationally known economist who later would go to the U.S. Senate, argued strongly against this provision, calling it "in part a confusion of the idea of relief with that of insurance." He explained his point: "The workers will have made direct contributions for half of their annuities and indirectly they will have paid for most of the employers' as well. When the system is thoroughly established, they will have therefore earned their annuities. To require them to give up gainful employment is, in reality, attaching a condition upon insurance which they themselves have bought."

As it turned out, Social Security was stripped of its character as an "insurance program" from the start. The contributions made by the employer and employee were not vested in an account for the worker, despite appearances to the contrary. As a result, the earnings penalty was only one way in which a worker could lose benefits which he or she had earned. If a worker died, either his survivor's benefits would be reduced, or if he had no survivor, the benefits would be lost, absorbed by the system itself.

The earnings test was designed to discriminate against the very people who most need to continue to receive benefits—the elderly poor. Social Security rules provide that "unearned" income, such as funds from interest, dividends, or rent, is not counted as income for the purpose of determining whether benefits will be cut. Wealthy retirees, even those with multimillion-dollar portfolios, continue to be eligible for benefits. However, a poor person with no assets can be severely penalized if he attempts to increase his income by taking a job.

The discouragement to work potentially affects an enormous number of people. In 1977 there were over thirty-four million receiving some benefits under the Old Age, Survivors, and Disability Insurance (OASDI) program. Most of these people are retirees who are not likely to try to remain in the work force beyond the age at which they can expect to begin receiving benefits. In fact, recent studies show that the decision to retire is most often determined by eligibility for benefits.

Under current law, a Social Security beneficiary under sixty-five begins to lose benefits when his income goes above $5,500. When the Social Security retiree has earned any money above this ceiling, he loses one dollar of benefits for each two dollars of earnings. In other words, the "tax" on Social Security benefits is higher than the standard income tax on earned income. What's more, the retiree with earned income must pay income taxes on that income. As a result, the effective tax rate on earned income may be as high as 60 or 70 percent. As we have seen, the 67 percent "tax" on welfare acts as a discouragement to work. The same is true for Social Security.

The social cost of the work disincentive built into Social Security is also high. Highly skilled older workers are deliberately forced from the labor market by the threat of jeopardizing the "pension" for which they have worked all their lives.

I recall a visit I once made to a U.S. senator to urge him to support a bill which would have removed the earnings limitation. As I began to argue my case, he interrupted to tell me that he had already decided not only to support the bill, but to cosponsor it. He had been moved to take this action, not by arguments such as mine, but by his own poignant personal experience.

Some years earlier, his father had been suffering from terminal cancer. He was cared for by a nurse who had cared for several other members of his family over the years. After having tended to the bedridden man for some months and having achieved some success in easing his pain, she said she would have to quit. She told the senator that she would reach sixty-two within a week and that she wanted to begin drawing Social Security benefits. In fact, she did not really want to retire, but since she was eligible for benefits, she did not want to work for less than what she felt was her due. She left the bedside of the senator's father when she had earned the basic limitation. With evident sadness, the senator told me that shortly after the nurse had left his home, his father had died—alone.

The retirement incentive in Social Security is strong. At the time when Paul Douglas complained about it, this inducement was rationalized as a means of opening job opportunities for younger workers and thereby cutting depression-era unemployment.

This belief has persisted in good times and in bad. It

runs directly counter, however, to the trend toward longer life and the desire of a great many older people to continue to make a productive contribution to the American economy. Indeed, Congress has begun to fight against the discrimination that the elderly have faced when they have attempted to continue to work. Federal law now bars mandatory retirement at age sixty-five. However, the effect of such moves has already been undermined by the retention of the work disincentive of the Social Security program.

Pressure to induce early retirement has also done much to create the severe financial problems faced by Social Security. Since it is now possible to retire with reduced benefits at age sixty-two, and as retirees have lived more years after they have stopped working, the financial burden imposed by these retirees has increased. At the same time, the number of younger workers from whom contributions can be expected has not grown as once anticipated. The net result is that Social Security is a very faulty income-transfer program; income is insufficient to balance the long-term burden of outlays. Even so, in 1977 the total benefits paid exceeded $80 billion.

In addition, the Social Security trust fund itself has been dragged into political controversies concerning the federal budget. Originally, funds involved in Social Security were kept segregated from the general budget. But in the 1960s, when President Johnson wanted to accentuate the share of the budget devoted to domestic social purposes (and simultaneously to lessen the proportionate share of the Vietnam War), the Social Security accounts were made part of the general budget.

The program's financial woes have developed despite the influx of "windfall" income into the system. With the tremendous growth of illegal alien workers, Social Security has received at least $500 million a year in contributions from these people. Yet there is almost no chance that they will be authorized to draw benefits at a later date. In fact, they obtain illegal Social Security numbers because they try to mislead employers into believing that they are legal workers, not because they expect to receive benefits.

Paradoxically, despite the mounting costs of Social Security, the program has still left a sizable number of older Americans classified as poor. In 1978, 13.9 percent of all elderly people had incomes below the poverty line. In part, this state of affairs is due to the belief that Social Security would serve as the principal pension for retirees, although, at the outset, it was designed to be only a supplementary retirement plan.

In actuality, Social Security is not working as intended, and it is serving to promote the wasteful dependency system instead of strengthening the free enterprise system. The steps that should be taken to alleviate this situation are equally obvious.

First, the elderly ought to be assured of the dignity which comes from being self-supporting, if they choose to be, and government ought to encourage them to opt for a productive life as long as possible. Accordingly, the high benefit reduction rate applied to Social Security when a beneficiary manages to earn some money is counterproductive and morally wrong. It ought to be changed.

Second, the method of financing Social Security should be changed. Social Security's funding should be drawn from general tax revenues. In that way, it would be supported by the income tax, which is certainly more progressive than today's Social Security payroll tax.

Third, Social Security benefits should be subject to the income tax. At first glance, this may seem to involve the imposition of even more taxes on the incomes of the elderly poor. In actual practice, the benefits paid to such people would not be sufficiently high to require them to pay taxes on their income. On the other hand, the wealthy who may have earned Social Security benefits but who, because of sizable additional income, do not really need them would not be allowed to keep all they receive. As a result, the taxation of Social Security would cause benefits to be distributed more progressively. Benefits would be more in line with need, and the overall cost of the program would be reduced.

The problem with the way Social Security rules have been designed and applied is that, all too often, they seem to be completely indifferent to human needs. Take, for example, the case of a seventy-year-old Florida master clock repairman and watchmaker. Although crippled by rheumatoid arthritis, the man continued to repair clocks in his home. Social Security officials warned him that his monthly check of $115.80 would be reduced because he was exceeding the earnings limitation. Depressed that he would have to give up the only work that provided him with a reason to live, he wrote a farewell note to his sister and then took poison. Here we have the case of a man literally killed by the diligent application of the rules.

Disability Insurance: The Blank Check

Perhaps the single greatest explosion in federal spending for a social-welfare program has come in the Social Security disability assistance. Just a few years ago, this program covered relatively few people at a relatively modest cost. In 1965, 1.6 million people received $1.5 billion in benefits. The program seemed to be a reasonable one. A person who was physically or mentally disabled and who had previously worked under Social Security could be eligible for disability payments that made up for lost income. The disability would have to be serious and long-term, because benefits would not be payable during the first five months of a person's inability to work. After that waiting period, payments would be made directly to the disabled person, in cash, to be used however the recipient desired. By 1978 more than five million people were benefiting from this insurance and costs had climbed to $15 billion a year.

What happened with disability insurance at that point is almost a classic study of manipulation of public assistance programs by the use of eligibility rules.

President Carter proposed that eligibility and benefit rules be tightened in an attempt to bring costs under control before recipients became too wedded to their generous benefits. For example, he proposed that total benefits for a beneficiary and his or her dependents should not be more than 80 percent of the worker's average earnings. Some workers were actually finding it more advantageous to be disabled than to work.

Carter's proposal contained a number of work incentives. The unusual expenses that a disabled person might incur in preparing to return to work could be deducted from earnings, so that merely working enough to cover these expenses would not result in a loss of benefits. He proposed that the nine-month trial work period, during which a worker would not lose his or her eligibility for disability payments if the job proved too burdensome, be extended to twenty-four months. Medicare would be extended to cover people who had gone back to work and had been dropped from disability coverage.

These proposals recognized that the potential for abuse lay in the failure of the disability program to provide adequate work incentives. It was almost certain that the rapid growth in the number of people receiving benefits and in the huge sums spent was due, in part, to the attractive benefit levels, coupled with the absence of work incentives.

At the same time that Carter was asking for steps that would save money and encourage the disabled to work, the Social Security Advisory Council, a group sympathetic to the needs of less fortunate people, was presenting its proposals for additional coverage that would cost $4.1 billion more a year. Their request reflected the attitude of those who thought that the federal government was actually being too stingy.

The council proposed that the waiting period be reduced from five months to three months. It suggested that the requirements for prior work under Social Security be eased. Other recommendations called for making it easier for the wives or widows of disabled workers to obtain more benefits. The cost of these changes would be borne by a Social Security fund that was already in serious trouble.

No one would suggest that we do not have a special obligation to help those who have worked hard and who are now disabled. But we must also be sure that only the truly disabled receive any such special assistance. Yet there are serious problems in the practical application of these good intentions. Not only is there considerable pressure gradually to increase the number and kinds of people who can receive benefits, but it is difficult to determine just who is disabled and for how long.

Determining eligibility, even in the case of a blind person, can be an awesome task. An acquaintance of mine became blind as a result of a condition related to diabetes. After participating in an extensive rehabilitation program, he decided to learn computer programming so that he could begin a new career in which blindness would not be a major impediment.

When he started to look for a job, his caseworker told him that he could lose his Social Security disability benefits. If he took a job and held it for more than nine months, he would be considered to have no disability and would cease to be eligible for coverage. Nevertheless, the newly handicapped man talked with me about a job. I made clear I would be happy to offer him one. I recognized that he was capable and diligent. Eventually, however, he decided that he could not accept the job unless I could guarantee it for him for the rest of his working life, perhaps even if my company stopped using computers or went out of business. He worried that if he accepted the job, he would never again be eligible to receive blindness benefits. He finally decided that taking the job was too much of a risk.

Once again, the rules were acting as a barrier to work. Once again, pressure groups, genuinely concerned with the well-being of people in need, were demanding even greater benefits that could only strengthen the dependency system. Once again, the absence of a comprehensive program of income support had led to a makeshift policy and its almost instant inequities.

CHAPTER 6

The Compensations
of Unemployment

A few years ago, a twenty-two-year-old New York City
woman working as a package wrapper for a Manhattan
department store collected a salary of $3.00 per hour or
$120.00 for a forty-hour week. She was single and had no
dependents. When she collected her paycheck at the end of
each week, she found that no fewer than five different kinds
of deductions had eaten away at it:

Social Security	$7.26
Federal income tax	12.70
State income tax	3.40
City income tax	1.55
New York disability	.30

The check was made out for only $94.79. Worse yet,
getting even that small paycheck cost her money, because
she had to pay $2.00 a day for bus and subway transporta-
tion. Lunch cost her an average of $2.50 a day, and coffee
breaks took another seventy cents a day. These work-

related expenses amounted to $26.00 a week, leaving her only $68.79 to spend.

If she had been unemployed, she would have received $60 a week. As it was, she calculated that she was actually netting less than that. If she had been jobless, she would not have had to buy new clothing.

Although she told herself that she enjoyed working, she decided that she would be foolish to continue. Once she came to that decision, all else flowed automatically. She knew she could not collect unemployment insurance if she quit her job. Accordingly, she set out to get herself fired. A twenty-six-week paid vacation would be well worth it, she felt.

Because this happened some time ago, the amounts seem small. The discouragement to work was provided by the combined impact of all those taxes and the approximate equality of unemployment benefits and net income.

The Social Security Act of 1935 established an unemployment insurance system in the United States for the first time. The program was designed to work on a cooperative basis between the federal government and the states; and it still operates that way. The federal government levies a nationally uniform payroll tax on employers to finance the Unemployment Trust Fund. The tax rate is currently 3.4 percent of the first $6,000 of each employee's wages. State payroll taxes also provide for support for unemployment benefits, and the federal government has increasingly been called upon to contribute to them from general revenues. During the 1974–75 recession, twenty-four states depleted their trust-fund reserves and had to borrow from the federal government to pay jobless benefits. By early 1980, $13 billion of their debt was still outstanding. Each state sets its own benefit levels, which consequently vary widely among the states.

Unemployment benefits normally last for twenty-six weeks, but they may be extended for two additional thirteen-week periods if there is substantial unemployment. Federal money reimburses the states for part of their spending for such extended benefits. In addition, those people who remain unemployed after the end of extended benefit eligibility may find that they can turn to one of many programs of public assistance or of public-service employment. As a result, once a person begins to receive unemployment benefits, he or she may, in fact, be entering the dependency system.

Unemployment insurance has two purposes. First, it provides workers with a financial cushion when they are involuntarily thrown out of work. Second, by keeping money flowing into the economy through the hands of those who are temporarily unable to earn their own money, unemployment insurance serves to counteract the forces of economic slowdown.

The problem of unemployment insurance is that it succeeds too well in meeting these purposes. It can replace such a large part of a worker's paycheck that it discourages him or her from looking for a new job.

As the case of the New York package wrapper indicated, there may also be little incentive for the unemployed to stay on the job. A recent report by the federal government's General Accounting Office well illustrates the problem. In a survey of unemployment recipients, GAO found that nearly one-fourth were receiving more than 75 percent of their net working income. Moreover, 7 percent were actually receiving more from unemployment compensation than they had taken in as net wages when they had worked.

The explanation for this discrepancy, GAO says, lies in the tremendous growth of taxes since 1935. Most states continue to mandate unemployment compensation at 50 percent of gross wages—up to a certain maximum. Nevertheless, federal and state taxes today take a high percentage of whatever the wage earner is paid. In addition, the costs of getting to work and of day-care have soared. Thus, unemployment compensation set at 50 percent of gross wages can actually amount to a far higher percentage of the jobless worker's former net wages.

GAO points out that the ratio of unemployment compensation to past net wages has a real influence on a person's determination to find a new job. Jobless persons whose unemployment compensation equaled 75 percent or more of past net wages stayed unemployed longer than those with a less favorable ratio.

For some seasonal or occasional workers, unemployment compensation serves a "rest of the time" subsidy. For instance, some people in seasonal occupations—such as those catering to tourists—are content to work hard during a small part of the year in return for high earnings. Then they sit back and accept unemployment payments, knowing they will be able to work again at the beginning of the next busy season. By averaging their unemployment benefits and their elevated seasonal pay, they can end up with a decent annual income.

This willingness to make the most of unemployment compensation has a major impact on the economy. Harvard economist Martin Feldstein has estimated that the national unemployment rate is increased by three-quarters of one percent because of the work disincentive built into unemployment insurance.

To be sure, an unemployed worker drawing benefits is expected to be available for employment. Administrative rules require, as a condition of receiving benefits, that he or she make an effort to find work. Sometimes, state employment offices refer people to prospective employers, and recipients undertake job interviews in order to continue to receive payments. No one denies, however, that the work requirement really is something of a sham. An unemployed person can be obliged to accept a job only if it is in the field in which he or she has been working and if it is offered at a pay level equal or superior to the one he had previously enjoyed. These restrictions offer a most convenient way for a person who does not want to work to refuse offered jobs. In fact, some economists believe that the "work requirement" is completely illusory and that the unemployment of people receiving benefits should be categorized as altogether voluntary.

Probably all skilled workers could immediately be placed in positions requiring fewer skills, but almost all refuse to accept such assignments. This is particularly true of workers who have a good prospect of getting their old jobs back. For example, factory workers, laid off for extended periods, almost always prefer to live on unemployment benefits rather than to accept a lower-paying job until they can go back to their original positions.

For what may be as many as a million or more people, unemployment insurance serves as a source of second income; they also earn money from the nation's thriving "off the books" subterranean economy. Economist Peter M. Gutmann, who has done much research on the dynamics of the subterranean economy, has pointedly summed up how so many "unemployed workers" behave:

"The government naively takes for granted that such workers will tell about their work status with 'gospel' truth. But there is a great deal of incentive to do otherwise. Put bluntly, plenty of respondents lie; they lie consistently, and they lie with good reason. Will someone collecting welfare benefits, who has been required to register employment as a condition for receiving such benefits, tell the . . . interviewer that he is, in fact, not looking for work? Of course not! He knows that he is supposed to be tossed out of the program if he fails to look for work."

The cost to the economy of an unemployment policy which has no effective work incentive is high. Unnecessarily bloated unemployment rolls drain millions of dollars from the trust fund. When this situation becomes acute, general-revenue funds must be used to supplement and extend benefits, and all working taxpayers must then bear the burden. In short, the work of millions, including that of many who have valuable skills, is denied to producers.

Even more significantly, the unemployment insurance mechanism serves to enhance the distinction between the free enterprise society and the dependency system. By its operations, millions of people leave the ranks of the employed to accept government subsistence payments. While it might be argued that many of them will ultimately go back to work, the cumulative effect at any one moment can be staggering. In 1978 more than ten million people received unemployment payments. Some were truly out of work and unable to find acceptable jobs. Others, however, had actively sought to be fired so that they would be eligible for benefits, or they had no intention of looking for work until the time when they would automatically lose benefits.

The human cost is also enormous. Yes, the despair and frustration of a person genuinely unable to find work is emotionally crippling. But perhaps even more damaging to character and an individual work ethic is the acquiescent acceptance of unemployment insurance as an income replacement when the recipient has relatively little interest in an early return to work.

A woman, for example, once wrote a letter to the *New*

York Times in which she described the unemployment-insurance program—of which she was a beneficiary—as "an unending stream of financial aid for anyone who can figure out a way of working only when he wants and collecting the rest of the time." Reporting on her own experience, she said, "Physically, my energy was never lower. I felt listless much of the time. Mentally, I was in a fog, confused and wandering, not wanting to focus on what was happening in my life. I was half-alive, unable and unwilling to fulfill my responsibilities as an adult, to take care of myself, to give to my community." Unemployment insurance has thus radically changed this woman's personality, and the change would make it more difficult for her to be an attractive candidate for employment.

The Private Sector: Promoting Dependency

Needless to say, the government is not solely responsible. Certain practices in private business also help to create unemployment. One flagrant abuse in the private sector is coming to an end. I refer to the pernicious practice of mandatory retirement. By forcing employees to retire at a specified age, business has created much dependency among people who wish to continue productive lives.

In 1978 Congress passed a bill banning mandatory retirement below the age of seventy. While this was a healthy step, I believe that forced retirement at any specific age should be prohibited. Retirement should be a matter of mutual negotiation.

Our national economy needs the productivity that mature workers offer. Many wish to retire at sixty-five, to be sure. But others want to continue to be productive, to keep busy, and to earn their incomes, often at the highest levels of their careers. The experience of older workers is a precious resource that America should protect.

In my own company, the chief engineer wanted to cut down his workload, but did not want to retire. We worked out a schedule for him that benefited him, the company, and his fellow workers. He was made a company vice-president and given a part-time schedule for part-time pay. He represented the company with customers and suppliers and in regard to acquisitions. We were able to offer the position of chief engineer to a promising candidate as our employment solicitation. The younger workers achieved more rapid advancement, and the company did not lose the benefit of its chief engineer's experience. As for the older man, the part-time schedule allowed him to serve on the school board in his community and gave him the leisure to build a retirement home.

A few years ago, the IBM Corporation, which has its headquarters near our plant, announced a mandatory retirement policy for senior executives at the age of sixty. I took a small ad in the local newspaper:

FACING COMPULSORY RETIREMENT?

COME TO SAFE FLIGHT.

WE EVALUATE ABILITY, NOT BIRTHDAYS.

The ad received an overwhelming response. One executive in his forties called me. I said, "You're not facing mandatory retirement." He replied, "Ever?"

The legislation prohibiting mandatory retirement below the age of seventy has many loopholes. One allows the forced retirement of employees who have accumulated pension rights worth over $20,000 a year. This exemption was obviously targeted at senior executives who are often the most talented workers. It makes no sense to forgo their ability.

The law also does not prohibit retirement incentives, which often make a voluntary decision to retire an economic imperative for a worker. Such practices as early-retirement bonuses make it difficult for a worker to continue on the job even if he wants to. Offering a bonus to a worker to retire at the age of fifty-five makes a mockery of the law supposedly prohibiting mandatory retirement at that age.

Another tactic used to get around the law is the canceling of pension credits at a certain age. A company may have a pension program, but if the program's benefits do not continue to accumulate after the worker reaches sixty-five, the employee's incentive to go on working is considerably reduced.

Social Security and other retirement benefits woo many workers into retirement each year by destroying work incentive. It is no wonder that we are running out of funds for Social Security. It is time that the nation recognized the contribution these workers can continue to make.

Another widespread abuse in the private sector is the easy availability of disability benefits. Today, a worker with a hard-to-confirm complaint, such as a back injury, can receive disability pay almost indefinitely. Whereas in former days such a worker would have had an incentive to switch to a different type of work and contribute to national productivity, he now finds it possible to receive as much as 90 percent of his salary by staying home. The cost of these programs is passed on to the employer's insurer, who must charge higher premiums to everyone. Instead of protecting workers against disability, these generous benefits often throw them into dependency and lives of idleness.

CHAPTER 7

The War
to End Welfare

Nobody knows who coined the phrase "welfare mess," probably because it became so obvious to so many people at the same time. The system that Franklin D. Roosevelt had introduced—somewhat reluctantly and in the belief that it would be phased out at the end of the depression—kept right on growing. Neither the boom times of World War II nor the policies of the fiscally conservative Eisenhower administration dispelled the growing dependence of Americans on the "benefits" dispensed by their government.

As it grew, welfare became more complex. The welfare bureaucracy became larger. The number of constituencies with vital interests in the welfare system increased. Somewhere along the line, depression relief became the welfare mess.

By the mid-1960s, conditions seemed ripe for doing something to eliminate the mess. The nation enjoyed a long period of economic health during the 1950s and early 1960s. Steady gains gave hope of genuine progress for every part of our economy. President Kennedy seemed to promise that as he called for intensified economic growth with an old chestnut: "A rising tide lifts all boats."

The War on Poverty

Lyndon Johnson not only shared Kennedy's hopes for the revival of the economy and the reduction of poverty, he actually came to see the elimination of poverty in strong moral terms as well. The United States should not acquiesce in continued poverty at the same time that it was growing increasingly wealthy. Some of that wealth must be used to eliminate poverty.

Perhaps even more important, Johnson simply did not see that the welfare system by its very nature *perpetuates* poverty. What the Texan lacked in economic sophistication, he more than compensated for by the strength of his belief in (1) the possibility of change and (2) the power of money to effect such changes. If the poor could be given needed skills and made more employable through education and training and if their living conditions improved, then the requisite billions would be allocated to see that it happened. Poverty would be eliminated! The effort would be costly, he fully recognized. Nevertheless, he saw the expenditure as an investment that needed to be made only once. It would later yield handsome dividends in the form of reduced welfare spending and increased income-tax receipts.

The promise was extravagant. "We have never lost sight of our goal, an America in which every citizen shares all the opportunities of his society," he said. "To finish that work, I have called for a national war on poverty. Our objective: total victory." Launched in the early months of the Johnson Administration, when the national sentiment had rallied around the president, the War on Poverty met with widespread support.

In less than five years, federal aid to the poor doubled. At the outset of the War on Poverty, spending totaled almost $12 billion. By 1969 it had reached more than $24 billion. While the considerable dollar growth had taken place in cash assistance to the poor, the largest percentage increases were in programs designed to improve their skills, their education, and their health.

At the center of the "war" effort was the Office of Economic Opportunity (OEO), originally headed by R. Sargent Shriver, the brother-in-law of John F. Kennedy. The OEO was lodged in the White House in order to demonstrate the highest level of support for its programs, and it eventually came to coordinate a plethora of new approaches to reducing poverty. Shriver, taking Johnson at his word, sought massive federal financing for the effort to improve economic conditions for the poor. In 1966 he submitted a five-year plan that called for $28 billion for OEO itself and another $152 billion for such antipoverty programs as manpower development and training, education, and Food Stamps.

Among the OEO programs was Community Action, which would employ the poor themselves to work on projects designed to reduce poverty. To match the exhilarating initiative of the Peace Corps, a parallel domestic effort, known as Volunteers in Service to America (VISTA), was begun. The more fortunate and skilled who volunteered for this program were sent, not to underdeveloped areas abroad, but to urban ghettos and rural poverty pockets.

Considerable attention was also paid to preparing the poor to take paying jobs. The Job Corps and the Neighborhood Youth Corps were the focal points of this effort, and they received financing of $576 million in 1966 alone.

Other OEO programs were admittedly more long-term in their intended effect and concentrated on educational programs. Head Start focused on preparing the disadvantaged poor for their entry into elementary school. In effect, it said that middle- and upper-class children had cultural advantages and that it was up to the government to compensate for the lack of these advantages among the poor. At the other end of the spectrum, Upward Bound took on the task of preparing poor youth for college.

One of the most innovative elements of the OEO approach was a program of legal services for the poor. Based on the belief that only through access to the legal system could the poor protect themselves against economic discrimination, it stirred controversy by assisting the disadvantaged in bringing law suits against the very economic interests whose taxes supported the antipoverty effort.

Foster Grandparents and Green Thumb tapped the abilities of older Americans to care for institutionalized children and improve their communities. Other OEO activities focused on help for American Indians and migrant workers.

Bureaucratic Problems

All of these programs were administered directly from the White House by OEO, much to the displeasure of traditional government agencies that wanted jurisdiction. At the same time, OEO had the responsibility of coordinating all other poverty-related programs provided by the federal government.

Instead of vaulting over the administrative problems of the traditional welfare program by establishing new and far-reaching ways of dealing with the problems of the poor, the OEO was soon mired in a bureaucratic morass—which contributed even more confusion and waste.

For its entire existence, the OEO had to fight off efforts to break it up and distribute its programs among traditional agencies. Johnson defended the OEO during the time he was in office; President Nixon whittled the office down and, in time, split up its functions.

Without a doubt, the Community Action program brought many of the poor into leadership positions and gave them the skills they would later use in politics, social action, and even business. But the great number of opportunities that existed far outstripped the available supply of talented but disadvantaged people. As a result, as the *National Journal* later reported, "many inexperienced, unskilled persons suddenly found themselves administering large government programs and couldn't cope with the bureaucratic tangle or the fine points of the law."

Because of the sudden creation of these leadership slots and the inability of Washington to structure them carefully, the new managers, just out of poverty, were called upon to define their own tasks, a responsibility often beyond their abilities. There was considerable waste and a stupendous misuse of funds. Community projects became laden with scandal. The "povertician" was soon recognized as a new breed of plunderer. Rather than being in the hands of the archetypal political boss, graft was now in those of the "community leaders" placed in control of the local poverty program.

Although disenchantment with the OEO grew and the promise of the War on Poverty was not fulfilled, many new programs from the era survived. Even before the OEO was moved out of the White House and converted into the independent Community Services Administration, other

programs had been shifted elsewhere. Head Start and Upward Bound were placed under the Department of Health,
Education, and Welfare in 1970. The Job Corps went to the
Labor Department in 1970; the Neighborhood Youth
Corps had already done so in 1965. Ultimately the Neighborhood Youth Corps was abolished. VISTA and Foster
Grandparents became a part of ACTION, an umbrella organization that included the Peace Corps and other voluntary programs.

The geographic site of the nation's greatest concentration of poverty was shifting. President Johnson saw it as
being in the South and in other rural areas. As a result, he
focused his war effort there. But population shifts were
under way which would change the very nature of the poverty problem.

The cities, with their higher welfare benefits and apparent economic strength and diversity, attracted millions
from the rural areas, especially from those in the South. In
1959 some 56 percent of the people living below the poverty line inhabited rural America. By 1977 these areas ac-
counted for only 40 percent of the poor. To be sure, a
substantial number of the poor still remained in rural areas
—a disproportionately large number, in view of the relatively small part of the total population that lived in those
areas. Still, more than four-fifths of the reduction in poverty between those years was the result of its drop in rural
areas. Meanwhile, the share of the poor who lived in central
cities rose sharply, mostly as a result of migration. The
army of the War on Poverty thus constantly had to be
redeployed to take into account the population shift.

Furthermore, there was more to the reduction in poverty in the rural South than could be explained by migration. Although the poorest states continued to be there, the
region began a period of sustained economic growth at just

about the same time that Johnson targeted it for aid. New industry meant new jobs. Not only did the out-migration slow, but skilled young people from other regions began to take advantage of the new opportunities. Poverty was thus reduced by economic expansion and by the replacement of the poor, many of whom went elsewhere, by more affluent people from other parts of the country.

Johnson's War on Poverty had little impact on these developments. In fact, the efforts started under his administration may actually have served to slow the move back to the South. High welfare and unemployment benefits in the industrial North may have encouraged the poor to stay put and accept public assistance, rather than to pull up stakes and head for new opportunities in the South.

Ironically enough, studies on the economic impact of public assistance programs, weapons in the arsenal of Johnson's war, indicate that they have had the least impact in the South. A report by Sheldon Danziger and Robert Plotnik of the Institute for Research on Poverty at the University of Wisconsin has revealed that about half of the poor were lifted above the poverty line by cash transfer benefits (though in-kind benefits are not counted here). By contrast, only about 30 percent of the poor in the South were similarly affected. This differential was caused in large part by the lower benefits that the southern states provided.

Critics of Johnson's war also suggest that the decision to establish jobs programs where the poor were concentrated actually contributed to the programs' ultimate failings. The poor were often found in large numbers in areas stagnating economically. While public jobs provided them with employment rather than with welfare benefits, such jobs had very little chance of leading to gainful employment in the private sector. Opponents of Johnson's approach argued that it would be wiser to site public-service jobs in areas of higher growth, so that they would serve as a transition from welfare to work in the private sector.

In addition, the wide publicity given the War on Poverty actually contributed to its problems. A great many people who were eligible for welfare or other forms of public assistance had not been aware of their rights before the War on Poverty. When they learned about the requirements for AFDC, millions of welfare mothers went onto the rolls, as was their right. Suddenly, the magnitude of the problem seemed to increase.

Another reason for the failure of the War on Poverty was the very design of some of the elements of the program. Hopes that turned out to be too high were vested in plans such as Head Start, the Jobs Corps, and Community Action. At the same time, some of these efforts were never funded at the levels Johnson had foreseen.

In Johnson's own terms, the war was lost. He intended that it would be a massive, only temporary effort leading to a reduction in poverty through gainful employment. The figures tell a disappointing story. In 1965, without taking into account public assistance, 21.3 percent of the population was poor. In 1976, again ignoring both cash and in-kind benefits, we find nearly 21 percent of the population still below the poverty line. Clearly, almost one-fifth of our national population is now in what appears to be permanent dependency. What have we loosed upon our society?

The Growth of the Dependency System

Increased dependency has had a pervasive impact on American political and social life. Taxpayers, called upon to foot an ever increasing bill for public assistance, have become properly resentful. Public-opinion surveys repeatedly show that most people put welfare-cost reduction as their highest priority in cutting government spending. They are outraged by the burgeoning bureaucracy, by the mounting cost and the seeming intractability of the problem.

At the same time, the poor are no happier! The net result of the antipoverty effort appears to be the demoralization of the poor.

One of President Johnson's principal objectives has been lost, too. He intended to fulfill Roosevelt's goal of gradually phasing out public assistance programs as the poor moved into productive jobs. The new operations launched in the War on Poverty were only seen as means to this end. Yet, in the end, almost all of them survived the war effort and were simply added to the list of income transfer programs. As a result, the welfare mess grew larger.

The impact of benefits programs on the American economy did change significantly, however. In 1965, transfer payments—such as welfare, Social Security, and unemployment compensation—amounted to 7.6 percent of total personal income. By 1976 they had risen to 14 percent of it. This trend explains in part Congress's difficulty in getting control of the federal budget. Income transfers came to be regarded as uncontrollable parts of the budget, not subject to annual pruning. As a result, the part of the budget over which Congress had discretion decreased each year.

CHAPTER 8

The Struggle to Reform Welfare

The problems in the welfare system that I have identified have always been present in the legislation since the enactment of the Social Security Act of 1935. But even though the work disincentives were there, they were not apparent until the mid-1960s when the Great Society expanded welfare. Only after the initiatives of President Lyndon B. Johnson did the nation begin to realize how costly, in both human and financial terms, welfare could be.

As the War on Poverty brought welfare dependency to millions of new clients, it also spawned a nationwide search for improved methods of reducing poverty. It is a tragedy that none of the reforms has ever been adopted, because the longer the welfare system remains intact, the more people it will ensnare and the more costly it will become. In reviewing the history of the many attempts at welfare reform undertaken in the sixties and seventies, I do not aim to accuse anyone of bad faith or bad judgement. Recriminations are pointless. But an objective review of these events will help us to avoid the mistakes that were made.

The first noteworthy thrust at welfare reform came from an unlikely source. In 1962 the conservative economist Milton Friedman proposed scrapping welfare and replacing it with a negative income tax (NIT). The NIT would create an automatic government payment to any family whose income fell below a certain point. The amount of the payment would vary with earnings, but the family would always have more money by working than by not working.

NIT received its first official endorsement when R. Sargent Shriver, the first director of OEO, called for its enactment. NIT was a compelling approach that broke new ground. But it contained many of the flaws of the system it was intended to replace. First, NIT starts at a level close to the poverty line, creating a distinction between tax payers and tax receivers. Also, it has a high marginal tax rate, over 50 percent, which is not sufficient to instill work incentive. To be sure, NIT is not a categorical program, but it is only a small improvement.

Shriver was not joined by many other liberals in calling for welfare reform, so Johnson decided to appoint a presidential commission to study the matter. With this move, Johnson effectively pushed the thorny question of welfare reform over to the next administration. The commission was headed by the railroad president Ben Heineman. Its report, handed to newly elected President Richard Nixon, called for a negative-income-tax approach.

Nixon, during his campaign, had promised welfare reform but had not specified a program. In the early days of his administration, responsibility for devising a plan went to his domestic counselor Daniel Patrick Moynihan, a Democrat who had served in subcabinet positions in the Kennedy and Johnson administrations. The result of intense administration deliberations was the Family Assistance Plan, a hybrid of the negative income tax and children's allowance. FAP was a categorical program in that it applied only to families with children. It had a high marginal tax rate and a benefit level that welfare-rights groups considered too low. In short, FAP had enough flaws to create a coalition of diverse opponents that doomed it from the start. I took out a full-page ad in the *New York Times* carrying the headline:

> "Nixon's Family Assistance Plan . . .
> ONE STEP ACROSS A TWO STEP DITCH?"

FAP quickly passed the House of Representatives. The going was considerably tougher in the Senate, where Russell Long, the chairman of the powerful Finance Committee, announced his early opposition.

I testified before Senator Long's committee. I was displeased with the high marginal tax rate. I told the committee of the work disincentive inherent in the plan. I suggested that the personal income tax exemption could be made refundable. If it were then scaled into the basic FAP benefit, I testified, it would reduce the marginal tax rate to an acceptable level.

The testimony which immediately preceded mine offered a classic example of constituency power and the obstacles it presents. It was given by the head of the National Association of Social Workers. He made it very clear that his union would fight against the enactment of any reforms that entailed an attrition in the number of required social workers.

FAP's high benefit-reduction rate was its greatest difficulty. Even though the welfare rights groups opposed the Nixon plan on the ground that its benefit level was too low, George Wiley, the head of the National Welfare Rights Organization told me in a private conversation that he was more interested in work incentives than in high benefits. At the time, his group had the slogan "$5,400 or fight." But

Wiley said to me, "If there was a stronger work incentive, I'd settle for half."

And although Senator Long's rhetoric stressed his dislike of the income guarantee that he saw in FAP, he made his most telling points when he attacked the plan on its work disincentive. When HEW Secretary Robert Finch testified before the Finance Committee, Senator Long asked him to explain the fact that a family earning $3,000 would net more money than a family earning $3,500. Finch had no answer. Long thundered, "Go back! Go back and do your homework!" Finch was replaced by Elliot Richardson. Richardson smoothed the notches out of FAP, but that left it with so little work incentive that it made little difference what one earned at a level of less than $7,500 per year—down to not working at all.

After FAP failed to make it through the Senate, President Nixon determined that it could—and must—pass in a slightly modified version in the next session of Congress. At that time, my office became a sort of clearinghouse for proponents of welfare reform.

FAP passed the House again, but the presidential campaign of 1972 intervened and killed any chance that meaningful welfare reform might have had at the time. I had refined my plan into what I called Fair Share. It had many supporters in Congress, both liberals and conservatives. It was the first widely recognized plan to make use of the tax-credit strategy. Sen. George McGovern of South Dakota, the leading contender for the Democratic presidential nomination, adopted part of my plan in his welfare reform program. But his failure to include a key element of Fair Share—the proviso that it *replace* existing welfare programs—sealed McGovern's doom and had even bigger implications for the future of welfare reform in America.

McGovern's leading opponent was former Vice-President Hubert H. Humphrey of Minnesota, the 1968 Democratic nominee who had since been reelected to the Senate. Humphrey was a supporter of the existing welfare system, in the creation of which he had had a large part. He seized upon McGovern's plan—a $1,000-per-capita demogrant—as a massive giveaway.

The key test of the political viability of McGovern's plan came in the California primary. The polls showed that McGovern was leading by a margin of two to one over Humphrey. A debate was scheduled in May which analysts thought would be decisive. I called McGovern's campaign manager, Frank Mankiewicz, and told him that McGovern would be questioned on his plan's cost. I said that I had worked out the figures and would be glad to provide them. Mankiewicz replied, "Oh, no, thank you. We have a team of Ivy League experts working on it."

During the debate, Humphrey challenged McGovern, "What will your plan cost?" McGovern said, "I don't know." Humphrey shot back, "Well I'll tell you what it will cost—over $60 billion." McGovern was devastated.

Had McGovern's plan been intended to replace the existing welfare structure, it would have saved money. In fact, only that month I had placed advertisements in the California newspapers headlined,

"HOW WELFARE REFORM CAN SAVE THE
AVERAGE TAXPAYER MONEY."

But McGovern's refusal to make this element a part of his program allowed Humphrey to portray it as another costly scheme that voters were seeking to avoid. McGovern's poll ratings plummeted. By August, he had dropped welfare reform from his campaign agenda.

Once welfare reform had thus been removed from the campaign, President Nixon felt no political need to push the issue. FAP was not reintroduced, and welfare reform never again received the intense national attention that it had gotten in the early 1970s.

This was a shame because it was an issue that could have united many factions in the political spectrum. For example, welfare reform could have brought the organized-labor movement closer to the liberals and conservatives in both parties from whom labor had become estranged. At about the time of the 1972 California primary, I wrote to AFL-CIO President George Meany about my Fair Share plan. He replied, "Your plan presents the simple, universal justice that labor must achieve."

Meany asked for a meeting to discuss Fair Share. I relayed this request to McGovern. He responded that they were winning in California and with that behind them, they had no need for Meany. The words "We don't need Meany" did more to lose him the election than any other act.

On the other hand, winning business support for welfare reform turned out to be an easier task. After the election, the Chamber of Commerce of the United States decided to study the welfare problem from a business point of view. I was invited to the chamber's Council on Trends and Perspectives, at which we began an in-depth study of various approaches to welfare reform. The council opted for the tax-credit approach because it offered the greatest incentive to entry-level labor, which was in short supply because of the welfare system.

For the balance of the Nixon and Ford administrations, welfare reform was put "on the back burner." Aides at HEW were busy working on new plans. One of them, called the Income Security Plan, was pushed very hard by HEW Secretary Caspar Weinberger. But President Ford refused to introduce it, and its details were never even made public until Weinberger left office and released his proposal in an article in *The Journal/The Institute for Socioeconomic Studies.*

In early 1976 The Institute sponsored a conference in Washington at which Senator Humphrey was to present his Humphrey-Hawkins "full employment" bill. I formed a panel for questions. One of the panelists was former Congresswoman Martha Griffiths, a leading proponent of welfare reform. Before an audience of national leaders, she questioned Humphrey very closely on the work incentives in his bill. When she pointed out that many people affected by it would receive no net benefit from employment, Humphrey waffled. It seemed to me that the time was ripe for welfare reform to be a major issue once again in a presidential campaign.

President Jimmy Carter did make it one of his leading issues. But when his administration took office, internal disputes over the design of his plan led to the adoption of a compromise approach called the Program for Better Jobs and Income. (Renamed from the Better Jobs and Income Program, which formed a bad acronym!)

Carter's main difficulty was high unemployment in 1977. He felt that he could not seek a comprehensive welfare reform if the private sector could not provide jobs to the poor. His plan set a national minimum benefit for AFDC and set up a large program of public-service jobs.

Administration officials met with me, and I told them of my displeasure with the Carter bill. They said that it was not possible for a comprehensive plan to pass Congress.

Since the bill did meet some of my major objections to the existing welfare system, I decided to support a modified version. I testified before the House and Senate Public Assistance Subcommittees that the bill was a good first step and deserved to be considered. But Congress became enmeshed in a dispute over the cost of the Carter plan, and the latter never came to a vote.

In the aftermath of the defeats of Nixon's FAP and Carter's PBJI—and despite the measures that Congress had adopted independently of the two proposals—it appeared that the welfare mess might have to be regarded as a permanent part of the American political and economic landscape. The period since the launching of Johnson's War on Poverty had been characterized by deep concern about the shape of the welfare system, but also by the lack of political will or inventiveness to come up with an alternative. As a result, the United States remained a nation divided. For some, there was the continued promise of the free enterprise system. For others, the dependency system had clearly become a fixture. The failure of FAP and the PBJI offered new proof that any comprehensive reform had to represent a significant break with the ways of thinking that had been born during the New Deal.

CHAPTER 9

Energy Aid:

A New Example of
Welfare Proliferation

As the impact of soaring energy costs threatened to place a new financial burden on the nation's poor and elderly, policymakers were faced with the challenge of creating a new public assistance program. At the same time, public willingness to spend more money on the poor in the form of energy aid offered a new hope that imaginative approaches could be developed to replace the stale and unworkable welfare mechanisms of the past.

Although nowhere near as large as Medicaid or other rapidly growing welfare programs, energy assistance would entail between two and three billion dollars a year when federal and state aid programs were taken into account. Funding of this magnitude would allow for significant increases in benefits.

The Federal Programs

By 1976 political leaders recognized that rising prices of home heating oil, the result of the Arab oil embargo and the subsequent producer-price spiral, could mean serious hardships for the poor and elderly. If those living on low and fixed incomes were forced to juggle their small budgets to pay fuel bills, they might have to forgo other essentials. If they did not reorient their budgets, they might suffer through a long, cold winter. The media carried horror stories of older people whose frozen bodies had been found in their homes, after they had run out of funds to pay for oil deliveries. The fear grew that people would have to choose between heating and eating.

As a result of such stories, a public which would have opposed any new welfare program and politicians who would have considered it suicidal to vote for such a program suddenly found themselves eager to provide help to those most threatened by rising fuel prices.

The original energy aid program in 1976 was designed to last one year and to tide the poor over in a winter during which fuel prices rose at an unexpectedly rapid rate. Presumably, if such sharp increases did not continue, people would be given breathing space to reorient their family budgets and welfare administrators would be able to adjust benefits to take into account increased heating costs. But prices did not level off, and repeated sudden price jumps led to a growing recognition that energy aid would have to be continued.

By the fiscal year 1980, it was evident that federal energy assistance had become permanent. Congress had adopted a windfall-profits tax on the oil companies in order to recover some of the gains that would accrue to them as a result of price decontrol. Because Congress recognized that decontrol would mean higher prices for the heating-oil consumer, it decided that some of the proceeds of the windfall-profits tax would have to be allocated to helping the poor and elderly meet those higher prices.

During the winter of 1979–80, the federal government earmarked $791.2 million in energy aid to AFDC recipients and an additional $404.8 million to SSI beneficiaries. The payments to those eligible under SSI took the form of direct lump-sum payments by the federal government to individuals. Under this program, some SSI beneficiaries received unneeded energy assistance, because they were not responsible for meeting fuel costs. When some state officials suggested that these people should sign over their energy aid checks to their landlords, they met with a solid wall of resistance. In the following year, Washington decided to allow states the option of doling out benefits to SSI eligibles in an effort to avoid a repetition of this situation.

The payments to AFDC recipients were distributed through block grants to the states. Such an approach had long been favored by conservatives unhappy with the current welfare system. They had argued that state governments were closer to the people than was Washington and could thus better tailor benefits to local needs, and in line with local values.

Under the block grant system, each state can determine the exact amount of assistance that will go to each recipient, although it is required to provide the greatest amount of help to those with the lowest incomes. But that is not the only guideline for the distribution of such aid. The assistance may be used only for home-heating costs and, when medical circumstances indicate, for air-conditioning costs. Benefits may be paid either directly to those eligible or to energy suppliers, as well as to operators of subsidized housing. Many states have chosen to channel the aid to suppliers as a way of insuring that it is used for the intended purpose. States may also allocate up to 3 percent of the federal funds to a reserve fund to be used in case of especially severe weather conditions. Up to 5 percent may be used for the costs of administering the program, provided that the state allocates a matching amount for that purpose. The states are also required to create a mechanism for monitoring the program in order to insure that aid goes only to those who are eligible.

Each state can decide which families will receive energy aid. To be eligible, the recipient must pay some of the energy costs and must have an income below a limit established by the federal government. Either the household income must fall below the lower living standard of the Bureau of Labor Statistics or the family must include at least one member eligible for AFDC, SSI, or other public assistance. The BLS standard was adopted for use beginning in 1981; it replaced an earlier ceiling set at 125 percent of the poverty level.

While each state must designate a single agency that is to administer the program, it can turn the actual distribution of money over to local groups. Such subcontracting of responsibility has itself created problems, because local agencies have sometimes favored their usual client population without always inquiring into actual need. In addition, although the block grant approach is supposed to prevent the creation of an even larger federal welfare bureaucracy, the complex regulations imposed on the states have served simply to transfer the growth of red tape from the federal to the state and local levels.

The real battle in Congress concerning the energy aid program for the poor was neither over its establishment

nor over the shape it would take. Instead, in a classic example of pork-barrel politics, Congress spent most time wran-
gling over the allocation of the available aid among the
states. Although the avowed original intention of the program was to get help to the poor in states where the climate
was the most severe, the ultimate decisions have reflected
a test of political strength pitting the North and East a-
gainst the South and West. While funds for Hawaii, Texas, and
Louisiana have been sharply boosted, increases have been
far more modest for Maine, New Hampshire, New York,
and Washington. Rep. Silvio O. Conte, a Massachusetts
Republican, said that the program had "gone bananas."

Still, the program is expected to continue to grow, with
more gains for those states with the least need. In the fiscal
year 1980, some 17.1 million people were eligible, but a
year later that number had risen to 20.7 million.

The low-income energy-assistance program, administered by the Department of Health and Human Services, is
earmarked exclusively for fuel costs and cannot be used for
conservation measures which would actually reduce energy
consumption. To the recipient, energy aid simply represents an increased level of welfare benefits.

The Department of Energy has operated an entirely
separate energy aid program, also aimed mainly at meeting
the needs of the poor. This program, which provides for
assistance in home weatherization, is designed to reduce
energy consumption and hence is expected to control
spending for fuel. In 1977 some $490.5 million was al-
located for a multiyear weatherization effort. But it lagged,
because DOE entangled it in a web of regulations so complex that states preferred not to use the available funds. For
example, the rules required that only CETA and volunteer
labor could be used. But such labor was in short supply.
Eventually, in hopes of increasing the pace of weatheriza-

tion, DOE eased the rules and allowed contractors to be hired when CETA people are unavailable.

Still another attempt by the federal government to help the poor deal with rising energy costs was the Public Utilities Regulatory Policies Act (PURPA), enacted in 1978. This law requires agencies that regulate state utilities to review a series of mechanisms which might reduce the cost of electricity or natural gas for low-income users, but it does not compel them to adopt any mechanism.

PURPA involves little expenditure of public funds. Instead, it represents a kind of income redistribution through the mechanism of utility rates. Public utilities must acquire their operating revenues from the rates charged users. If they are to be required to lower rates for poor users, the revenue loss will have to be made up through higher rates for other classes of users. The small amount of federal funding involved in the program is to be used to subsidize intervention in rate cases before state utilities commissions by representatives of the poor. But the main thrust of the law is redistribution.

Patchwork: The States Respond

Because of a belief that federal aid would be inadequate in the face of extreme weather conditions or simply because of a concern that federal aid would arrive too late in the winter season, many states have adopted their own energy aid programs. In 1979–80, some fourteen states had such programs. The largest was in New York, where $143 million was appropriated and where the state sales tax on home heating oil was removed.

In some states, officials believed that those with incomes just above the federal cut-off line would also experience hardship in paying fuel bills unless they received some public assistance. In addition, they worried about a middle-class backlash against energy aid that was earmarked exclusively for the poor.

As a result, several states have instituted programs to provide for assistance to those above the cut-off line. Some provide for cash payments on behalf of those whose household incomes range up to 150 percent of the poverty line. And at least one state went so far as to subsidize low-interest weatherization loans for people with incomes as high as $22,000.

Most of these state programs are operated as supplements to the federal aid and are administered by the same agencies that are responsible for handling the federal programs. Consequently, the state efforts have not been involved in any innovative approaches to the distribution of public assistance. Instead, their programs appear to be a mosaic of stopgap measures.

Almost all of the efforts to provide energy assistance have suffered from the drawbacks already associated with categorical welfare programs. Criteria for obtaining benefits from various public assistance programs frequently conflict. Overlapping cut-off points where benefits are lost have severely penalized recipients who have found jobs—thereby creating strong work disincentives. The welfare bureaucracy has continued to grow.

Less cumbersome and more effective possibilities have been ignored. The proceeds of the windfall-profits tax were allocated to an energy aid program burdened by mechanisms similar to those which had already been discredited and by a distribution formula influenced more by the political pork barrel than by a concern with efficiency. The remaining windfall-tax revenues were to be used to help reduce the enormous federal budget deficit, and thus they served to lessen the need for reducing government waste, instead of being channeled back to the people.

Do not be alarmed at the prospect of reading the enormous list that follows. It is included at this point only for visual impact. Listed are the names and amounts of the income transfer programs as of 1977. This list was taken from the inventories of federal, state and local income transfers as published by The Institute for Socioeconomic Studies.

The example given in this chapter is meant to show how we reached this welfare proliferation. A mess indeed!

PROGRAMS

Title: SUPPLEMENTAL SECURITY INCOME, Administering Body: Social Security Administration, Department of Health, Education & Welfare, Cost: $5,299 million (Fiscal 1977 est.). TITLE: EXCLUSION OF PUBLIC ASSISTANCE BENEFITS, Administering Body: Internal Revenue Service, Department of Treasury, Cost: $100 million (Fiscal 1977 est.). Title: AID TO THE AGED, BLIND AND DISABLED, Administering Body: Social and Rehabilitation Service, Department of Health, Education & Welfare, Cost: $5 million (Fiscal 1977 est.). Title: ADDITIONAL EXEMPTION FOR THE BLIND, Administering Body: Internal Revenue Service, Department of Treasury, Cost: $20 million (Fiscal 1977 est.). Title: ADDITIONAL EXEMPTION FOR THE AGED, Administering Body: Internal Revenue Service, Department of Treasury, Cost: $1,220 million (Fiscal 1977 est.). Title: CREDIT FOR THE ELDERLY, Administering Body: Internal Revenue Service, Department of Treasury, Cost: $495 million (Fiscal 1977 est.). Title: SOCIAL BENEFITS FOR PERSONS AGE 72 AND OVER, Administering Body: Social Security Administration, Department of Health, Education & Welfare, Cost: $236 million (Fiscal 1977 est.). Title: SOCIAL SECURITY - RETIREMENT INSURANCE, Administering Body: Social Security Administration, Department of Health, Education & Welfare, Cost: $52,364 million (Fiscal 1977 est.). Title: EXCLUSION OF SOCIAL SECURITY BENEFITS, Administering Body: Internal Revenue Service, Department of Treasury, Cost: $4,240 million (Fiscal 1977 est.). Title: RAILROAD RETIREMENT INSURANCE, Administering Body: Railroad Retirement Board, Cost: $2,250 million (Fiscal 1977 est.). Title: EXCLUSION OF RAILROAD RETIREMENT BENEFITS, Administering Body: Internal Revenue Service, Department of Treasury, Cost: $200 million (Fiscal 1977 est.). Title: CIVIL SERVICE RETIREMENT PENSIONS, Administering Body: Civil Service Commission, Cost: $6,370 million (Fiscal 1977 est.). Title: MILITARY NONDISABILITY RETIREMENT, Administering Body: Department of Defense: Coast Guard, Department of Transportation, Cost: $7,233 million (Fiscal 1977 est.). Title: SENIOR COMMUNITY SERVICE EMPLOYMENT, Administering Body: Employment and Training Administration, Department of Labor: Cost: $74 million (Fiscal 1977 est.). Title: SENIOR OPPORTUNITIES AND SERVICES, Administering Body: Community Services Administration, Cost:$11 million (Fiscal 1977 est.). Title: FOSTER GRANDPARENT PROGRAM, Administering Body: ACTION, Cost: $40 million (Fiscal 1977 est.). Title: SENIOR COMPANION PROGRAM, Administering Body: ACTION, Cost: $9 million (Fiscal 1977 est.). Title: SOCIAL SECURITY - DISABILITY INSURANCE, Administering Body: Social Security Administration, Department of Health, Education & Welfare, Cost: $11,625 million (Fiscal 1977 est.). Title: RAILROAD DISABILITY INSURANCE, Administering Body: Railroad Retirement Board, Cost: $551 million (Fiscal 1977 est.). Title: VETERANS COMPENSATION FOR SERVICE-CONNECTED DISABILITIES, Administering Body: Department of Veterans Benefits, Veterans Administration, Cost: $4,796 million (Fiscal 1977 est.). Title: VETERANS PENSIONS FOR NON-SERVICE-CONNECTED DISABILITIES, Administering Body:

Department of Veterans Benefits, Veterans Administration, Cost: $1,870 million (Fiscal 1977 est.). Title: EXCLUSION OF VETERANS PENSIONS AND DISABILITY COMPENSATION, Administering Body: Internal Revenue Service, Cost: $685 million (Fiscal 1977 est.). Title: CIVIL SERVICE DISABILITY PENSIONS, Administering Body: Civil Service Commission, Cost: $1,694 million (Fiscal 1977 est.). Title: DISABLED COAL MINE WORKERS BENEFITS AND COMPENSATION, Administering Body: Social Security Administration, Department of Health, Education & Welfare and Employment Standards Administration, Department of Labor, Cost: $935 million (Fiscal 1977 est.). Title: EXCLUSION OF SPECIAL BENEFITS FOR DISABLED COAL MINERS, Administering Body: Internal Revenue Service, Department of Treasury, Cost: $50 million (Fiscal 1977 est.). Title: MILITARY DISABILITY RETIREMENT, Administering Body: Department of Defense; Coast Guard, Department of Transportation, Cost: $980 million (Fiscal 1977 est.). Title: EXCLUSION OF MILITARY DISABILITY PENSIONS, Administering Body: Internal Revenue Service, Department of Treasury, Cost: $105 million (Fiscal 1977 est.). Title: LONG-SHOREMEN'S AND HARBOR WORKERS' COMPENSATION, Administering Body: Employment Standards Administration, Department of Labor, Cost: $6 million (Fiscal 1977 est.). Title: FEDERAL EMPLOYEES COMPENSATION BENEFITS, Administering Body: Employment Standards Administration, Department of Labor, Cost: $589 million (Fiscal 1977 est.). Title: EXCLUSION OF WORKER'S COMPENSATION BENEFITS, Administering Body: Internal Revenue Service, Department of Treasury, Cost: $705 million (Fiscal 1977 est.). Title: EXCLUSION OF SICK PAY FOR THE DISABLED, Administering Body: Internal Revenue Service, Department of Treasury, Cost: $50 million (Fiscal 1977 est.). Title: HANDICAPPED ASSISTANCE LOANS, Administering Body: Small Business Administration, Cost: $13 million (Fiscal 1977 est.). Title: SOCIAL SECURITY-SURVIVORS INSURANCE, Administering Body: Social Security Administration, Department of Health, Education & Welfare, Cost: $18,888 million (Fiscal 1977 est.). Title: RAILROAD SURVIVORS INSURANCE, Administering Body: Railroad Retirement Board, Cost: $1,026 million (Fiscal 1977 est.). Title: SURVIVORS COMPENSATIONS FOR SERVICE-CONNECTED DEATHS, Administering Body: Department of Veterans Benefits, Veterans Administration, Cost: $1,067 million (Fiscal 1977 est.). Title: VETERANS SURVIVORS PENSIONS, Administering Body: Department of Veterans Benefits, Veterans Administration, Cost: $1,322 million (Fiscal 1977 est.). Title: AID TO FAMILIES WITH DEPENDENT CHILDREN, Administering Body: Social and Rehabilitation Service, Department of Health, Education & Welfare, Cost: $5,718 million (Fiscal 1977 est.). Title: BURIAL ALLOWANCE FOR VETERANS, Administering Body: Department of Veterans Benefits, Veterans Administration, Cost: $150 million (Fiscal 1977 est.). Title: CIVIL SERVICE SURVIVORS PENSIONS, Administering Body: Civil Service Commission, Cost: $1,205 million (Fiscal 1977 est.). Title: MILITARY SURVIVORS BENEFITS, Administering Body: Department of Defense; Coast Guard, Department of Transportation, Cost: $120 million (Fiscal 1977 est.). Title: MEDICAL ASSISTANCE (MEDICAID), Administering Body, Social and

Rehabilitation Service, Department of Health, Education & Welfare, Cost: $9,859 million (Fiscal 1977 est.). Title: SOCIAL SERVICES, Administering Body: Social and Rehabilitation Service, Department of Health, Education & Welfare, Cost: $2,645 million (Fiscal 1977 est.). Title: STATE AND COMMUNITY PLANNING AND SERVICES FOR THE AGING, Administering Body: Office of Human Development, Department of Health, Education & Welfare, Cost: $140 million (Fiscal 1977 est.). Title: MEDICARE-SUPPLEMENTARY MEDICAL INSURANCE, Administering Body: Social Security Administration, Department of Health, Education & Welfare, Cost: $6,330 million (Fiscal 1977 est.). Title: MEDICARE-HOSPITAL INSURANCE, Administering Body: Social Security Administration, Department of Health, Education & Welfare, Cost: $15,314 million (Fiscal 1977 est.). Title: RETIRED FEDERAL EMPLOYEES HEALTH BENEFITS, Administering Body: Civil Service Commission, Cost: $433 million (Fiscal 1977 est.). Title: NUTRITION PROGRAMS FOR THE ELDERLY, Administering Body: Office of Human Development, Department of Health, Education & Welfare, Cost: $209 million (Fiscal 1977 est.). Title: EXCLUSION FROM CAPITAL GAIN ON HOME SALES BY THE ELDERLY, Administering Body: Internal Revenue Service, Department of Treasury, Cost: $40 million (Fiscal 1977 est.). Title: HOUSING FOR THE ELDERLY AND HANDICAPPED, Administering Body: Department of Housing & Urban Development, Cost: $262 million (Fiscal 1977 est.). Title: RENT SUPPLEMENTS, Administering Body: Housing Production and Mortgage Credit, Department of Housing & Urban Development, Cost: $245 million (Fiscal 1977 est.). Title: VERY LOW-INCOME HOUSING REPAIR LOANS, Administering Body: Farmers Home Administration, Department of Agriculture, Cost: $5 million (Fiscal 1977 est.). Title: SPECIALLY ADAPTED HOUSING FOR DISABLED VETERANS, Administering Body: Department of Veterans Benefits, Veterans Administration, Cost: $14 million (Fiscal 1977 est.). Title: VETERANS HOSPITALIZATION, Administering Body: Department of Medicine and Surgery, Veterans Administration, Cost: $2,862 million (Fiscal 1977 est.). Title: VETERANS CONTRACT HOSPITALIZATION, Administering Body: Department of Medicine and Surgery, Veterans Administration, Cost: $55 million (Fiscal 1977 est.). Title: VETERANS OUT-PATIENT CARE, Administering Body: Department of Medicine and Surgery, Veterans Administration, Cost: $872 million (Fiscal 1977 est.). Title: CIVILIAN HEALTH AND MEDICAL PROGRAM-VA, Administering Body: Department of Medicine and Surgery, Veterans Administration, Cost: $29 million (Fiscal 1977 est.). Title: VETERANS PRESCRIPTION SERVICE, Administering Body: Department of Medicine and Surgery, Veterans Administration, Cost: $12 million (Fiscal 1977 est.). Title: VETERANS PROSTHETIC APPLIANCES, Administering Body: Department of Medicine and Surgery, Veterans Administration, Cost: $50 million (Fiscal 1977 est.). Title: BLIND VETERANS REHABILITATION CENTERS, Administering Body: Department of Medicine and Surgery, Veterans Administration, Cost: $3 million (Fiscal 1977 est.). Title: VETERANS NURSING HOME CARE, Administering Body: Department of Medicine and Surgery, Veterans Administration, Cost: $147 million (Fiscal 1977 est.). Title: COMMUNITY NURSING HOME CARE, Administering Body:

Body: Department of Medicine and Surgery, Veterans Administration, Cost $75 million (Fiscal 1977 est.). Title: VETERANS DOMICILIARY CARE, Administering Body: Department of Medicine and Surgery, Veterans Administration, Cost: $69 million (Fiscal 1977 est.). Title: VETERANS GRANTS FOR STATE HOME CARE, Administering Body: Department of Medicine and Surgery, Veterans Administration, Cost: $36 million (Fiscal 1977 est.). Title: DEVELOPMENT DISABILITIES-BASIC SUPPORT, Administering Body: Office of Human Development, Department of Health, Education & Welfare, Cost: $32 million (Fiscal 1977 est.). Title: AID TO FAMILIES WITH DEPENDENT CHILDREN-UNEMPLOYED FATHER, Administering Body: Social and Rehabilitation Service, Department of Health, Education & Welfare, Cost: $400 million (Fiscal 1977 est.). Title: FEDERAL-STATE UNEMPLOYMENT INSURANCE, Administering Body: Employment and Training Administration, Department of Labor, Cost: $13,490 million (Fiscal 1977 est.). Title: RAILROAD UNEMPLOYMENT INSURANCE, Administering Body: Railroad Retirement Board, Cost: $183 million (Fiscal 1977 est.). Title: UNEMPLOYMENT COMPENSATION FOR FEDERAL CIVILIAN EMPLOYEES AND EX-SERVICEMEN, Administering Body: Employment and Training Administration, Department of Labor, Cost: $712 million (Fiscal 1977 est.). Title: EXCLUSION OF UNEMPLOYMENT INSURANCE BENEFITS, Administering Body: Internal Revenue Service, Department of Treasury, Cost: $2,745 million (Fiscal 1977 est.). Title: EXCLUSION OF EMPLOYER CONTRIBUTIONS TO SUPPLEMENTARY UNEMPLOYMENT INSURANCE TRUSTS, Administering Body: Internal Revenue Service, Department of Treasury, Cost: $10 million (Fiscal 1977 est.). Title: SPECIAL UNEMPLOYMENT ASSISTANCE, Administering Body: Employment and Training Administration, Department of Labor, Cost: $691 million (Fiscal 1977 est.). Title: TRADE ADJUSTMENT ASSISTANCE-WORKERS, Administering Body: Bureau of International Labor Affairs, Department of Labor, Cost: $254 million (Fiscal 1977 est.). Title: ECONOMIC ADJUSTMENT ASSISTANCE, Administering Body: Economic Development Administration, Department of Commerce, Cost: $30 million (Fiscal 1977 est.). Title: FEDERAL CROP INSURANCE, Administering Body: Federal Crop Insurance Corporation, Agricultural Stabilization and Conservation Service, Department of Agriculture, Cost: $67 million (Fiscal 1977 est.). Title: CRIME/RIOT INSURANCE, Administering Body: Federal Insurance Administration, Department of Housing & Urban Development, Cost: $2 million (Fiscal 1977 est.). Title: DAIRY AND BEEKEEPER INDEMNITY PAYMENTS, Administering Body: Agricultural Stabilization and Conservation Service, Department of Agriculture, Cost: $4 million (Fiscal 1977 est.). Title: COTTON PRODUCTION STABILIZATION PAYMENTS, Administering Body: Agricultural Stabilization and Conservation Service, Department of Agriculture, Cost: $108 million (Fiscal 1977 est.). Title: FEED GRAIN PRODUCTION STABILIZATION PAYMENTS, Administering Body: Agricultural Stabilization and Conservation Service, Department of Agriculture, Cost: $228 million (Fiscal 1977 est.). Title: RICE PRODUCTION STABILIZATION PAYMENTS, Administering Body: Agricultural Stabilization and Conservation Service,

Department of Agriculture, Cost: $135 million (Fiscal 1977 est.). Title: WHEAT PRODUCTION, Administering Body: Agricultural Stabilization and Conservation Service, Department of Agriculture, Cost: $111 million (Fiscal 1977 est.). Title: WOOL AND MOHAIR PAYMENTS, Administering Body: Agricultural Stabilization and Conservation Service, Department of Agriculture, Cost: $8 million (Fiscal 1977 est.). Title: EARNED INCOME CREDIT, Administering Body: Internal Revenue Service, Department of Treasury, Cost: $1,070 million (Fiscal 1977 est.). Title: EXCESS OF PERCENTAGE STANDARD DEDUCTION OVER LOW-INCOME ALLOWANCE, Administering Body: Internal Revenue Service, Department of Treasury, Cost: $1,285 million (Fiscal 1977 est.). Title: CREDIT FOR CHILD AND DEPENDENT CARE EXPENSES, Administering Body: Internal Revenue Service, Department of Treasury, Cost: $840 million (Fiscal 1977 est.). Title: EXCLUSION OF EMPLOYER-FURNISHED MEALS AND LODGING, Administering Body: Internal Revenue Service, Department of Treasury, Cost: $330 million (Fiscal 1977 est.). Title: EXCLUSION OF EMPLOYER CONTRIBUTIONS TO GROUP TERM LIFE INSURANCE PREMIUMS, Administering Body: Internal Revenue Service, Department of Treasury, Cost: $800 million (Fiscal 1977 est.). Title: EXCLUSION OF EMPLOYER CONTRIBUTIONS TO PENSION AND PROFIT-SHARING PLANS, Administering Body: Internal Revenue Service, Department of Treasury, Cost: $8,715 million (Fiscal 1977 est.). Title: EXCLUSION OF EMPLOYER CONTRIBUTIONS TO ACCIDENT INSURANCE PREMIUMS, Administering Body: Internal Revenue Service, Department of Treasury, Cost: $70 million (Fiscal 1977 est.). Title: EXCLUSION OF EMPLOYER CONTRIBUTIONS TO MEDICAL INSURANCE PREMIUMS, Administering Body: Internal Revenue Service, Department of Treasury, Cost: $5,195 million (Fiscal 1977 est.). Title: PUBLIC SERVICE EMPLOYMENT, Administering Body: Employment and Training Administration, Department of Labor, Cost: $3,159 million (Fiscal 1977 est.). Title: ECONOMIC OPPORTUNITY LOANS, Administering Body: Small Business Administration, Cost: $50 million (Fiscal 1977 est.). Title: SUMMER YOUTH EMPLOYMENT, Administering Body: Employment and Training Administration, Department of Labor, Cost: $595 million (Fiscal 1977 est.). Title: EMERGENCY ASSISTANCE TO NEEDY FAMILIES WITH CHILDREN, Administering Body: Social and Rehabilitation Service, Department of Health, Education & Welfare, Cost: $60 million (Fiscal 1977 est.). Title: INDOCHINESE REFUGEE ASSISTANCE, Administering Body: Social and Rehabilitation Service, Department of Health, Education & Welfare, Cost: $95 million (Fiscal 1977 est.). Title: CUBAN REFUGEE ASSISTANCE, Administering Body: Social and Rehabilitation Service, Department of Health, Education & Welfare, Cost: $68 million (Fiscal 1977 est.). Title: INDIAN GENERAL ASSISTANCE, Administering Body: Bureau of Indian Affairs, Department of Interior, Cost: $64 million (Fiscal 1977 est.). Title: VETERANS LIFE INSURANCE, Administering Body: Department of Veterans Benefits, Veterans Administration, Cost: $648 million (Fiscal 1977 est.). Title: EXCLUSION OF INTEREST ON LIFE INSURANCE SAVINGS, Administering Body: Internal Revenue Service, Department of Treasury, Cost: $1,815 million (Fiscal 1977 est.). Title: DISASTER ASSISTANCE, Administering Body: Federal Disaster Assistance Administration, Department of Housing & Urban Development, Cost: $387 million (Fiscal 1977 est.). Title: PHYSICAL DISASTER LOANS, Administering Body: Small Business Administration, Cost: $86 million (Fiscal 1977 est.). Title: FLOOD INSURANCE, Administering Body: Federal Insurance Administration, Department of Urban Development, Cost: $178 million (Fiscal 1977 est.). Title: DEDUCTIBILITY OF CASUALTY LOSSES, Administering Body: Internal Revenue Service, Department of Treasury, Cost: $345 million (Fiscal 1977 est.). Title: CRIPPLED CHILDREN'S SERVICES, Administering Body: Health Services Administration, Department of Health, Education & Welfare, Cost: $98 million (Fiscal 1977 est.). Title: FAMILY PLANNING PROJECTS, Administering Body: Health Services Administration, Department of Health, Education & Welfare, Cost: $121 million (Fiscal 1977 est.). Title: MATERNAL AND CHILD HEALTH SERVICES, Administering Body: Health Services Administration, Department of Health, Education & Welfare, Cost: $241 million (Fiscal 1977 est.). Title: MENTAL HEALTH-CHILDREN'S SERVICES, Administering Body: Alcohol, Drug Abuse and Mental Health Administration, Department of Health, Education & Welfare, Cost: $18 million (Fiscal 1977 est.). Title: COMPREHENSIVE SERVICES SUPPORT, Administering Body: Alcohol, Drug Abuse and Mental Health Administration, Department of Health, Education & Welfare, Cost: $132 million (Fiscal 1977 est.). Title: DRUG ABUSE COMMUNITY SERVICE PROGRAMS, Administering Body: Alcohol, Drug Abuse and Mental Health Administration, Department of Health, Education & Welfare, Cost: $159 million (Fiscal 1977 est.). Title: VETERANS REHABILITATION-ALCOHOL AND DRUG DEPENDENCE, Administering Body: Department of Medicine and Surgery, Veterans Administration, Cost: $107 million (Fiscal 1977 est.). Title: ALCOHOL COMMUNITY SERVICE PROGRAMS, Administering Body: Alcohol, Drug Abuse and Mental Health Administration, Department of Health, Education & Welfare, Cost: $56 million (Fiscal 1977 est.). Title: COMMUNITY MENTAL HEALTH CENTERS, Administering Body: Alcohol, Drug Abuse and Mental Health Administration, Department of Health, Education & Welfare, Cost: $79 million (Fiscal 1977 est.). Title: COMMUNITY HEALTH CENTERS, Administering Body: Health Services Administration, Department of Health, Education & Welfare, Cost: $229 million (Fiscal 1977 est.). Title: NATIONAL HEALTH SERVICE CORPS, Administering Body: Health Services Administration, Department of Health, Education & Welfare, Cost: $26 million (Fiscal 1977 est.). Title: INDIAN HEALTH SERVICES, Administering Body: Health Services Administration, Department of Health, Education & Welfare, Cost: $245 million (Fiscal 1977 est.). Title: MIGRANT HEALTH GRANTS, Administering Body: Health Services Administration, Department of Health, Education & Welfare, Cost: $32 million (Fiscal 1977 est.). Title: HEALTH MAINTENANCE ORGANIZATION DEVELOPMENT, Administering Body: Health Services Administration, Department of Health, Education & Welfare, Cost: $39 million (Fiscal 1977 est.). Title:

COMPREHENSIVE PUBLIC HEALTH SERVICES-FORMULA GRANTS, Administering Body: Health Services Administration, Department of Health, Education & Welfare, Cost: $95 million (Fiscal 1977 est.). Title: DEDUCTIBILITY OF MEDICAL EXPENSES, Administering Body: Internal Revenue Service, Department of Treasury, Cost: $2,585 million (Fiscal 1977 est.). Title: SPECIAL SUPPLEMENTAL FOOD PROGRAM (WIC), Administering Body: Food and Nutrition Service, Department of Agriculture, Cost: $248 million (Fiscal 1977 est.). Title: FOOD DONATIONS, Administering Body: Food and Nutrition Service, Department of Agriculture, Cost: $28 million (Fiscal 1977 est.). Title: SCHOOL MILK PROGRAM, Administering Body: Food and Nutrition Service, Department of Agriculture, Cost: $177 million (Fiscal 1977 est.). Title: NATIONAL SCHOOL LUNCH PROGRAM, Administering Body: Food and Nutrition Service, Department of Agriculture, Cost: $2,204 million (Fiscal 1977 est.). Title: SCHOOL BREAKFAST PROGRAM, Administering Body: Food and Nutrition Service, Department of Agriculture, Cost: $191 million (Fiscal 1977 est.). Title: SUMMER FOOD PROGRAM, Administering Body: Food and Nutrition Service, Department of Agriculture, Cost: $195 million (Fiscal 1977 est.). Title: CHILD CARE FOOD PROGRAM, Administering Body: Food and Nutrition Service, Department of Agriculture, Cost: $115 million (Fiscal 1977 est.). Title: COMMUNITY FOOD AND NUTRITION, Administering Body: Community Services Administration, Cost: $29 million (Fiscal 1977 est.). Title: FOOD STAMPS, Administering Body: Food and Nutrition Service, Department of Agriculture, Cost: $5,478 million (Fiscal 1977 est.). Title: LOWER INCOME HOUSING ASSISTANCE PAYMENTS, Administering Body: Housing Production and Mortgage Credit, Department of Housing & Urban Development, Cost: $362 million (Fiscal 1977 est.). Title: RENTAL HOUSING ASSISTANCE AND PAYMENTS, Administering Body: Housing Production and Mortgage Credit, Department of Housing & Urban Development, Cost: $527 million (Fiscal 1977 est.). Title: PUBLIC LOW-INCOME HOUSING, Administering Body: Housing Production and Mortgage Credit, Housing Management, Department of Housing & Urban Development, Cost: $1,112 million (Fiscal 1977 est.). Title: FARM LABOR HOUSING, Administering Body: Farmers Home Administration, Department of Agriculture, Cost: $7 million (Fiscal 1977 est.). Title: HOMEOWNERSHIP ASSISTANCE AND PAYMENTS, Administering Body: Housing Production and Mortgage Credit, Department of Housing & Urban Development, Cost: $148 million (Fiscal 1977 est.). Title: HOUSING REHABILITATION LOANS, Administering Body: Community Planning and Development, Department of Housing & Urban Development, Cost: $34 million (Fiscal 1977 est.). Title: RURAL SELF-HELP HOUSING TECHNICAL ASSISTANCE, Administering Body: Farmers Home Administration, Department of Agriculture, Cost: $6 million (Fiscal 1977 est.). Title: INDIAN HOUSING IMPROVEMENT, Administering Body: Bureau of Indian Affairs, Department of Interior, Cost: $14 million (Fiscal 1977 est.). Title: INDIAN SANITATION FACILITIES, Administering Body: Health Services Administration, Department of Health, Education & Welfare, Cost: $35 million (Fiscal 1977 est.). Title: EMERGENCY ENERGY CONSERVATION SERVICES, Administering Body: Community Services Administration,

Cost: $242 million (Fiscal 1977 est.). Title: FHA MORTGAGE INSURANCE, Administering Body: Federal Housing Administration Fund, Department of Housing & Urban Development, Cost: $647 million (Fiscal 1977 est.). Title: VETERANS HOUSING-GUARANTEED AND INSURED LOANS, Administering Body: Department of Veterans Benefits, Veterans Administration, Cost: $27 million (Fiscal 1977 est.). Title: HEAD START, Administering Body: Office of Human Development, Department of Health, Education & Welfare, Cost: $486 million (Fiscal 1977 est.). Title: LEGAL SERVICES FOR THE POOR, Administering Body: Legal Services Corporation, Cost: $125 million (Fiscal 1977 est.). Title: INDIAN SOCIAL SERVICES - COUNSELING, Administering Body: Bureau of Indian Affairs, Department of Interior, Cost: $9 million (Fiscal 1977 est.). Title: FEDERAL EMPLOYMENT FOR DISADVANTAGED YOUTH, Administering Body: Civil Service Commission, Cost: $105 million (Fiscal 1977 est.). Title: HIGHER EDUCATION WORK-STUDY, Administering Body: Office of Education, Department of Health, Education & Welfare, Cost: $250 million (Fiscal 1977 est.). Title: BASIC EDUCATIONAL OPPORTUNITY GRANTS, Administering Body: Office of Education, Department of Health, Education & Welfare, Cost: $1,461 million (Fiscal 1977 est.). Title: INCENTIVE GRANTS FOR STATE SCHOLARSHIPS, Administering Body: Office of Education, Department of Health, Education & Welfare, Cost: $32 million (Fiscal 1977 est.). Title: NATIONAL DIRECT STUDENT LOANS, Administering Body: Office of Education, Department of Health, Education & Welfare, Cost: $12 million (Fiscal 1977 est.). Title: HIGHER EDUCATION ACT INSURED LOANS, Administering Body: Office of Education, Department of Health, Education & Welfare, Cost: $484 million (Fiscal 1977 est.). Title: VETERANS DEPENDENTS EDUCATIONAL ASSISTANCE, Administering Body: Department of Veterans Benefits, Veterans Administration, Cost: $210 million (Fiscal 1977 est.). Title: VETERANS EDUCATIONAL ASSISTANCE, Administering Body: Department of Veterans Benefits, Veterans Administration, Cost: $3,683 million (Fiscal 1977 est.). Title: EXCLUSION OF VETERANS EDUCATIONAL ASSISTANCE, Administering Body: Internal Revenue Service, Department of Treasury, Cost: $255 million (Fiscal 1977 est.). Title: NURSING STUDENT LOANS, Administering Body: Health Resources Administration, Department of Health, Education & Welfare, Cost: $23 million (Fiscal 1977 est.). Title: HEALTH PROFESSIONS-STUDENT LOANS, Administering Body: Health Resources Administration, Department of Health, Education & Welfare, Cost: $20 million (Fiscal 1977 est.). Title: EXEMPTION FOR CHILDREN WHO ARE OVER AGE 18 AND STUDENTS, Administering Body: Internal Revenue Service, Department of Treasury, Cost: $750 million (Fiscal 1977 est.). Title: EXCLUSION OF SCHOLARSHIPS AND FELLOWSHIPS, Administering Body: Internal Revenue Service, Department of Treasury, Cost: $250 million (Fiscal 1977 est.). Title: UPWARD BOUND, Administering Body: Office of Education, Department of Health, Education & Welfare, Cost: $39 million (Fiscal 1977 est.). Title: SPECIAL SERVICES FOR DISADVANTAGED STUDENTS, Administering Body: Office of Education, Department of Health,

Education & Welfare, Cost: $20 million (Fiscal 1977 est.). Title: EDUCATIONAL OPPORTUNITY CENTERS, Administering Body: Office of Education, Department of Health, Education & Welfare, Cost: $3 million (Fiscal 1977 est.). Title: TALENT SEARCH, Administering Body: Office of Education, Department of Health, Education & Welfare, Cost: $5 million (Fiscal 1977 est.). Title: COMPREHENSIVE MANPOWER AND TRAINING SERVICES, Administering Body: Employment and Training Administration, Department of Labor, Cost: $1,414 million (Fiscal 1977 est.). Title: EMPLOYMENT SERVICE, Administering Body: Employment and Training Administration, Department of Labor, Cost: $614 million (Fiscal 1977 est.). Title: INDIAN EMPLOYMENT ASSISTANCE, Administering Body: Bureau of Indian Affairs, Department of Interior, Cost: $36 million (Fiscal 1977 est.). Title: MANAGEMENT ASSISTANCE TO DISADVANTAGED BUSINESSMEN, Administering Body: Small Business Administration, Cost: $7 million (Fiscal 1977 est.). Title: JOB CORPS, Cost: $230 million Body: Employment and Training Administration, Department of Labor, Cost: $365 million (Fiscal 1977 est.). Title: WORK INCENTIVE PROGRAM, Administering Body: Social and Rehabilitation Service, Department of Labor, Cost: $365 million (Fiscal 1977 est.). Title: REHABILITATION SERVICES AND FACILITIES - BASIC SUPPORT, Administering Body: Office of Human Development, Department of Health, Education & Welfare, Cost: $733 million (Fiscal 1977 est.). Title: VOCATIONAL REHABILITATION FOR DISABLED VETERANS, Administering Body: Department of Veterans Benefits, Veterans Administration, Cost: $104 million (Fiscal 1977 est.). Title: AUTOMOBILES AND ADAPTIVE EQUIPMENT-DISABLED VETERANS, Administering Body: Department of Veterans Benefits, Veterans Administration, Cost: $14 million (Fiscal 1977 est.). Title: VOCATIONAL REHABILITATION FOR SOCIAL SECURITY BENEFICIARIES, Administering Body: Office of Human Development, Department of Health, Education & Welfare, Cost: $93 million (Fiscal 1977 est.). Title: LOCAL PUBLIC WORKS EMPLOYMENT PROGRAM, Administering Body: Economic Development Administration, Department of Commerce, Cost: $520 million (Fiscal 1977 est.). Title: ECONOMIC DEVELOPMENT-PUBLIC WORKS, Administering Body: Economic Development Administration, Department of Commerce, Cost: $171 million (Fiscal 1977 est.). Title: COMMUNITY ECONOMIC DEVELOPMENT, Administering Body: Community Services Administration, Cost: $50 million (Fiscal 1977 est.). Title: COMMUNITY ACTION, Administering Body: Community Services Administration, Cost: $346 million (Fiscal 1977 est.). Title: VOLUNTEERS IN SERVICE TO AMERICA, Administering Body: ACTION, Cost: $23 million (Fiscal 1977 est.). Title: INDIAN CREDIT PROGRAM, Administering Body: Bureau of Indian Affairs, Department of Interior, Cost: $18 million (Fiscal 1977 est.). Title: NATIVE AMERICAN PROGRAMS, Administering Body: Office of Human Development, Department of Health, Education & Welfare, Cost: $42 million (Fiscal 1977 est.).

CHAPTER 10

Solving the Welfare "Mess"

The Graduated Income Supplement

One of America's favorite aphorisms comes from Mark Twain: "Everybody complains about the weather but nobody does anything about it." The same can be said for welfare.

While we Americans are willing to help our destitute neighbors, we have no desire to support a dependent class permanently. Yet our welfare system has not abolished poverty, and it has actually led to increased dependency. As a result, our actions seem increasingly irrelevant to reaching our goals, and discontent with welfare is almost universal, felt by both those who are dependent and those who pay.

To be sure, we have experienced periodic efforts at welfare reform. Some piecemeal measures have had a positive effect. But, more often, reform has consisted of more tinkering. The results, widely regarded as unsatisfactory, prove that tinkering can never be enough. In the meantime, the welfare system has become impossibly cumbersome to administer and intolerably expensive.

The Problems of Piecemeal Reform

Because of concerns about the potential cost and the resistance to innovation, some advocates of welfare reform argue that the most serious problems of welfare and the most pressing needs of the poor can best be met by relatively minor adjustments in current programs. They also emphasize the greater chances of political support for this approach than for more sweeping change.

Nevertheless, piecemeal reform, however politically attractive it may seem, cannot solve the deep-seated problems inherent in the welfare system. The essential reason for the inevitability of the failure lies with the origins of the system.

Historically, this approach bred the welfare monster by creating new programs every time a new perceived need was to be addressed. John L. Palmer, a senior fellow at the Brookings Institution, aptly compared the current welfare system to an old car. "The dilemma of welfare reformers reminds me of one I recently faced regarding my old, ailing automobile," he said. "It was built for conditions which no longer exist, so it could only meet some of my transportation needs. Over the years so many different mechanics had made ad hoc repairs and modifications that it resembled a Rube Goldberg creation. Although continued repairs would have kept it running, and perhaps even improved it,

it became clear that I could obtain a high level of perform-
ance by trading it in for a new model. We have come to the
same point with our welfare system."

While a "new model" is called for, it need not be
adopted all at once. It is possible to move toward fundamental reform in increments. What matters is the ultimate
goal. If the aim is a simple integrated program coordinated
with the tax system, it is realistic to approach this in stages.
The problem with the traditional approach is not that it has
been effected in stages but that the end result has been a
large number of categorical programs. The aim has not
been simplification and coordination.

Congress has never been willing or able to adopt what
we now call a zero-base approach to welfare, which would
strip away the layers of programs that have gradually been
added to the original concept. Instead, it has, by design or
by accident, created the welfare mess, which more of the
same will not eliminate.

Then too, one of the most undesirable results has been
the reality that many poor families have acquired eligibility
for several welfare benefits. Multiple eligibility virtually as-
sures that almost no family will receive the appropriate
amount of assistance or have its earned income properly
related to its public aid.

The family that tries to earn a paycheck can often find
that the "cost" of such an effort, one on which Americans
generally place great value, is so high that its members will
choose not to work.

Much of the deepest public resentment is reserved for
the welfare bureaucracy, whose growth is believed to have
gotten out of hand. Welfare critics see the bureaucracy as
actually serving to promote the welfare mess. A large bureaucracy is, of course, the inevitable outcome of establishing a host of categorical programs. Each agency must be-

come, to some extent at least, the captive of its own constituency. The process obviously erodes the agency's ob-
jectivity in its policy development. As the support of specific congressmen gravitates to the programs of given
agencies, there is a further lessening of the agency's ability
to do anything but "build its empire."

Take, for example, the case of the Food Stamp program. Originally intended as a surplus-commodity distribution scheme, it was lodged in the Department of Agriculture. However, the income transfer element of the program
has come to predominate, and it serves, at least for the
present, as the basic national guaranteed-minimum-
income program. Consequently, it would make more sense
to have the program administered by agencies within the
Department of Health and Human Services which are responsible for other aspects of welfare. In fact, with the
elimination of the purchase requirement for food stamps,
the program is a prime candidate for being "cashed out,"
for having its payments be made part of existing income-
support programs. Yet each time this suggestion is made,
the Agriculture Department and many farm-state senators
in Congress, succeed in blocking any consolidation. Still,
inclusion of food stamp benefits in other programs could
result in a reduction in the welfare bureaucracy. Perhaps
the fear of losing their jobs has been the most significant
factor in leading the existing bureaucrats in Agriculture
and other agencies to oppose efforts at welfare reform.

In short, a fragmentation of the government's benefits
programs has made the welfare mess much worse. Nothing
that furthers—or even maintains—this policy can be considered a part of a genuine reform program.

The Need for Comprehensive Reform

Any dispassionate study of welfare must inevitably lead to the conclusion that only a sweeping reform, replacing the current system completely, can end the welfare mess. Such broad reform immediately gives rise to serious concerns. Will a new program not be even more expensive? Will current recipients not lose their benefits? Will any comprehensive new program not be indifferent to the special needs of certain groups?

But these concerns can cause us to lose sight of an even more fundamental question: In view of the evidence that the current welfare system actually strengthens the dependency system, how can we hope for any significant improvement so long as we remain wedded to it? A reasonable answer to this question indicates the unavoidability of a comprehensive reform if we want to end the dependency system.

The forces arrayed against such a fundamental change are awesome. The welfare bureaucracy, out of sincere concern for current recipients, as well as for reasons of self-preservation, opposes such change as impractical. Congress resists, because it desires to cater to existing political constituencies. In addition, many members of Congress tend to support the very bureaucracies that they helped to create. Welfare constituencies have gained strength in recent years, thanks in part to the organizational impetus provided by Johnson's War on Poverty. These groups have shown themselves to be essentially interested in preserving the existing benefits of their members.

A proposal for comprehensive reform must take these groups into account. Undoubtedly any proposal will encounter substantial opposition from them, but it stands a chance of prevailing if it addresses the concerns they raise.

Despite the risks and perils, an effort must be made to replace welfare as we know it, before the present dependency system completely destroys the work incentive in our country and, because of the immense financial burden it puts on our economy, triggers violent upheaval.

A truly comprehensive plan for welfare reform must *(a)* include a work incentive; *(b)* promote the integrity of the family; *(c)* offer uniform benefits; *(d)* be integrated into our tax system; and *(e)* be easy to administer.

I therefore propose the Graduated Income Supplement (GIS), a mechanism which will meet all of these requirements, with the strength of great simplicity.

Every adult and, at a different level, every child is to receive a taxable income supplement. The dollar value of that supplement will be reflected on the income tax return as a reduction of taxes owed. If the amount of taxes owed is less than the supplement, a cash refund will be made. A family with no income will receive the full amount of the supplement in cash payments. Because the supplement is taxable income, its net value is progressive in accordance with the graduated income tax.

The Graduated Income Supplement will not call for a determination of the assets or the need of recipients. Its basic payments will be unrelated to any financial standard. However, thanks to taxation, it will operate as an income-related program.

The specific level of the tax credit need not be determined now. Benefit levels could be determined by the funds made available through the elimination of other welfare programs. In other words, the funds saved by fully or partially phasing out existing programs could be used to pay for the Graduated Income Supplement.

One virtue of the GIS is that it would absorb, in the reform, programs that are unrelated to need. What the United States now spends on the scores of income-maintenance programs of all kinds would be more than enough to fund the new programs at a level which would totally eliminate poverty.

Because of the gradual rise in tax rates as income increases, a family would not be unduly penalized for each added dollar of earnings. The gradual increase in taxation would insure that there would be no erosion of the work incentive. But, to reiterate, such a result could not be achieved without replacing the current welfare system with the Graduated Income Supplement.

The First Step: "Cashing Out"

The reform of welfare, broadly defined, depends on "cashing out" existing programs. The first step is to cash out in-kind benefits by assigning a cash value to the in-kind programs so that the new system can rest entirely on money payments to beneficiaries.

The evolution of the Food Stamp program indicates the course to be taken. At first, recipients of food stamps were required to pay cash for the stamps that would enable them to purchase what the government thought would be an adequate monthly diet. The purchase price was determined by need. As need decreased, the amount of food stamps that could be bought remained the same but the purchase price increased. If it was determined that a family of four required $200 per month, all such families in the program received $200 per month in stamps, but some paid nothing for them and some paid up to $195. In 1977 the program was changed to provide that people no longer had to pay for their stamps. Instead, as income rose, recipients were simply eligible to receive fewer stamps. They were expected to use their own funds to purchase the commodities necessary to bring their diet up to the minimum standards. The cashing-out process was not completed, however, because those stamps that are provided may still be used only to purchase food.

The reason for continuing in-kind benefits was the policymakers' concern that recipients would use cash benefits unwisely. After they had wasted their cash benefits, the argument went, they would return to the government to seek help in meeting their basic needs. The essence, then, of in-kind aid was governmental paternalism of the worst kind. It presumed that a bureaucrat would be better qualified to make decisions for the less fortunate.

With the cashing out of food stamps, they should be consolidated with the AFDC program. Most proposals for merging the two programs are based on the supposition that the funds from the Food Stamp program can be used to supplement and expand AFDC. While this is reasonable, given the size and longer history of AFDC, it would only tend to strengthen the unsatisfactory work disincentives of AFDC. In fact, it would be more constructive to blend AFDC into the Food Stamp system, which at least contains the essence of a graduated-income approach. There might be substantial problems in making such a shift, which would represent a major step toward comprehensive reform. But for that reason alone, and because no additional cost would be involved in such an undertaking, it would be well worth the effort.

In-kind programs have a long record of failure. For example, many public-housing programs have proven disastrous. The ultimate destruction of the Pruitt-Igoe project in St. Louis has, in fact, become symbolic of the failure of this approach. Today, housing programs rely on private developers, and the government is called upon to pay all or part of the recipient's rent. Still, the essential problem remains: people are restricted by government policy in their choice of where to live. Hundreds of thousands of sound housing units have been abandoned and fallen into neglect, because federal aid in the form of rent subsidies has gone to the rent-aided developments instead.

In-kind benefits almost always distort the market at which they are directed. The urban housing market for the poor is in shambles. Much of the skyrocketing cost of medical care can be attributed directly to Medicaid, the mammoth in-kind medical-aid program for the poor. Clearly, it has been overused and has invited fraud, with the result that medical costs for everyone in our society have increased.

After the first step of cashing out in-kind benefits has been taken, existing programs can be consolidated and replaced by a single comprehensive program.

The need for consolidation is apparent from any survey of the inventory of federal income transfer programs. There is no coherent theme to our income-support system, other than its failure to provide work incentives.

The absence of a coordinated approach has made it impossible for federal policymakers to evaluate the potential effects that the programs they adopt have on the national economy. Most significantly, economists have reported that the chaotic pattern of income-support policies makes it impossible to calculate the effect of any one of them on the distribution of national income. This finding buttresses the case for consolidation.

The Graduated Income Supplement provides a flexible approach to welfare reform. While the ultimate objective is comprehensive in scope, implementation can be accomplished on an incremental basis. The ultimate objective is to replace most of the existing $298 billion of transfers with the GIS. A reasonable method to adopt would be a gradual system of replacement, by which the GIS increases as additional programs are replaced.

Eligibility: Putting Everyone on the Same Footing

The Graduated Income Supplement would overcome the principal problem inherent in current welfare programs by providing for universal eligibility. Such a rule would virtually eliminate the potential for abuse.

The annual tax credit would be given to every adult. In addition, an annual tax credit in a lesser amount should go to every child without regard to the composition of any family. Eligibility requirements could thus be completely eliminated.

Under the Graduated Income Supplement, the poor would not have to arrange their lives so as to meet such requirements. The computer trainee would not have to quit his job in order to make his family eligible for a subsidized apartment. Fathers would not have to leave home to allow their families to qualify for AFDC. The elderly watchmaker would not be driven to despair by being forced to choose between benefits and work.

In addition, thanks to universal eligibility under the Graduated Income Supplement, the work incentive would be increased among the poor. No longer would a recipient who accepted a job face the prospect of an abrupt loss of benefits. A family would receive the tax credit whether or not it earned income. Under the current AFDC program, family benefits are reduced by the welfare "tax" of 67 percent. Because of the benefit reduction rates, a family may actually lose income when a member goes to work. With the Graduated Income Supplement, whose benefits would be subject to the usual income taxes, people would always find it worth more to work than to stay home and collect benefits.

Elimination of complex eligibility rules would eliminate the need for the tangled welfare bureaucracy and its complicated rules.

Much time, money, and effort have been spent on the eligibility folly by our mindlessly clinging to the tenet that benefits should go only to those in need. This belief has become so embedded in our thinking that what might be called "needism" has developed into one of the most significant obstacles to effective action to combat poverty.

To argue that welfare assistance should be provided without reference to need might seem paradoxical. The confusion results from a belief that because of our well-founded desire to help those in need, we must utilize a special mechanism for identifying such people. Instead of recognizing that we all participate in a single economic system in which some people are in need of the help of others, we act as though there were actually two separate systems with specific eligibility rules.

The division we have created between the needy and the providers of aid serves to stifle incentive. If a person seeks, through his own effort, to lift himself out of need, we strip him of his eligibility for assistance. This approach permits no gradual transition from need to self-support. As a result, official policy in the United States—a country supposedly dedicated to the work ethic—penalizes welfare recipients for almost any effort they make to get off the dole.

Does Supplementing Income Provide Work Incentives?

The concept underlying the Graduated Income Supplement is hardly new. Logic and experience indicate that by allowing money that is earned to serve as a supplement to welfare benefits rather than as an outright replacement for them, we will encourage people to work.

After President Johnson had decided against pushing for comprehensive welfare reform, his Commission on Income Maintenance Programs endorsed the concept of a negative income tax. It also favored the consolidation of welfare programs to achieve a greater work incentive. In the following years, a series of localized tests were conducted to study the effects of such an approach on work incentives. These tests were designed to provide data on how people receiving an income supplement would behave. It appears that such supplements led to no meaningful work reduction and that they may, in fact, have enhanced work incentives. In perhaps the most controversial of these studies, a tax rate of 50 percent was used, the highest that the IRS imposed on usual earned income. It is not surprising, then, that this study did not provide more positive results.

Still, there is some proof that people on welfare will work if it is profitable for them to do so. The existence of the "subterranean economy" is ample proof that people receiving welfare benefits will work provided they can keep all or most of that they earn. It demonstrates, perhaps better than any economist's argument, the bankruptcy of our current welfare policies.

Toward a National Standard

Today welfare programs are administered by the states, and some states even delegate administrative supervision to counties. Although the federal government is involved in almost every income-support program, it leaves the determination of the benefit levels and of some eligibility requirements to the states. Theoretically, this decentralized system allows each state to set benefits in line with the local cost of living and, to a certain extent, in accordance with the desires of the people in that state. The system, however, encourages wide and not always justifiable differences.

The inevitable result of wide disparities among states has been the disruptive phenomenon known as welfare migration. Poor people move from low-benefit states to areas offering more generous benefits, often without any regard to the higher cost of living in the states to which they move. Not all people relocate simply to get higher welfare benefits. Some do it in seeking work; however, they know that if they fail in that search, they can easily qualify for what seems to be a generous welfare benefit.

The benefit level provided under the Graduated Income Supplement would have to be the same regardless of a family's location. This requirement is imposed not only by the need to reduce migration but by the desirability of insuring an adequate income to all under a system that is so simple to operate that the welfare bureaucracies in the states can be dismantled.

In fact, a uniform national benefit level may encourage a beneficial kind of migration. The poor will be encouraged to move to areas where the cost of living is lower, and the opportunities for employment greater. The concentration of the poor in northern urban ghettos is the direct result of policies which have caused migration. Conversely, uniform benefit levels would almost certainly cause people to leave these centers of despair and dependency.

The Role of the Tax System

The twin imperatives of reducing the welfare bureaucracy and of providing a work incentive lead to the inescapable conclusion that income-support programs should be managed through the internal-revenue system. The most attractive aspect of the negative-income-tax proposal is that it would be integrated into the tax system. For a positive-income-tax proposal such as the Graduated Income Supplement, the advantages of this approach are even more evident.

Most significantly, the use of the income tax for taxing the earnings of welfare recipients would at once subject them to the same marginal tax rates that apply to everyone else and integrate them into the free enterprise system. Use of the same tax rates for the poor that are used for wage earners would provide a universal work incentive. By having one system for all people, we would free the poor from the demoralization that comes with being on the dole.

In effect, then, subjecting the earnings of the poor to the income tax and to no other welfare "tax" would amount to an increase in assistance for them. They would be able to keep more of what they earn and thus be more inclined to work.

The integration of the poor into the internal-revenue system implies, too, that their benefits must also be subject to income taxation. At first glance, this might appear to be taking back with one hand what was just given by the other. In fact, the low-income exemptions of the Internal Revenue Code, as it now exists, would serve to provide tax-free treatment for some or all benefits, depending on the income of the recipient. A poor family relying entirely on public assistance would thus not be likely to have to pay any taxes.

Exemption or favorable tax treatment relating to certain types of income is generally the result of congressional decisions to promote certain kinds of economic activity. Capital gains, for example, are taxed at a lower rate, and political contributions, up to a certain limit, are exempted. At the same time, it is abundantly evident that Congress has no wish to encourage people to seek public assistance. Consequently, the exemption of such benefits from income taxes runs counter to the philosophy that underlies special tax treatment of this kind.

Many income transfers are not related to need; as a result, government payments may go to people for whose exemption from taxation there is no economic justification. If, for example, a wealthy person received Social Security retirement benefits, it would be reasonable to subject those payments to income taxes. The poor retiree, heavily dependent on those payments, would probably not have to pay taxes on them. Common sense indicates that such a flexible approach is more desirable than the rigid rule which exempts all such benefits from taxation.

The integration of all income transfers into the tax system will result in the elimination of elements of the current system which discourage work, because it will provide a simple and fair method of reducing payments as income is earned. After all, we attempt to set income tax rates so that they will not destroy incentives among wage earners. Strong public sentiment opposes confiscatory taxes, and the tendency in recent years has been to lower the highest marginal tax rates. The logic underlying these moves is no less applicable to the poor than to the rich. The use of income tax rates to reduce benefits as income is earned would eliminate notches and break-even points which are unjust and which serve as powerful disincentives to work.

Administratively, the Internal Revenue Service could replace the welter of agencies and battalions of bureaucrats now employed in administering income-support programs, especially welfare. The IRS is today generally considered to be far more efficient than are agencies concerned with the administration of welfare. Each year it processes tens of millions of returns and collects and pays out billions of dollars. Because of the widespread belief in the efficacy of its enforcement system, the United States has one of the most efficient tax-collection systems, based mainly on voluntary action.

Administration by the IRS would be simple. Few changes in existing IRS procedures would be needed. It would have to institute monthly reports and payments for the long-term poor. The incentive for fraud would be reduced, because all persons would automatically be entitled to the Graduated Income Supplement.

The Economic Implications of the Graduated Income Supplement

No restaurant can function without dishwashers, and while illegal aliens wash our dishes, our poor citizens collect welfare. Apple farmers in New York certified that no domestic labor was available (at a time when unemployment was nearing 10 percent) in order to import foreign help.

Our people do not work productively. There is no incentive for them to take entry-level jobs. The burden imposed by the collective impact of millions of decisions to accept welfare rather than to work results in decreased productivity, the root of our nation's economic ills.

The chief effect of the Graduated Income Supplement would be to encourage the poor to work, to make their contribution to an increase in productivity.

Recent studies have shown that a significant cause of inflation in the United States is an inadequacy of supply in the supply-and-demand equation. Economic growth has been sought by stimulating demand. The public sector has been forced to assume the role of customer, and in the process it has drained capital from business and industry in order to pay for its burgeoning expenses. Potential private-sector employers find it increasingly difficult to acquire the capital necessary for the expansion which will create new jobs and produce more goods. This lack of productive capacity therefore limits supply and drives prices higher. Government competes with consumers for scarce supplies, prices rise, and foreign goods and workers move into the American market to fill the gap, at least in part.

The Graduated Income Supplement would serve to improve productivity by encouraging those in the dependency system to participate in the free enterprise system. Despite technological innovation, their labor is still desperately required and can, in fact, relieve business and industry of some of its reliance on scarce capital goods. The result should be an increase in supply.

In addition, the Graduated Income Supplement would reduce government spending on social-welfare programs, which constitute the fastest growing components of the public sector. If government outlays can be cut in this area, money can be released into the private sector through tax reductions and a decreased need for public borrowing. Capital that has been diverted from the private sector to finance huge federal deficits, to which social-welfare programs contribute, should be left in the hands of those who would use it to stimulate production, which would increase supply and thus slow inflation.

Our welfare system is an almost unique combination of the worst elements of government policy: it is wasteful, invites fraud, encourages idleness, and is intolerably expensive. The Graduated Income Supplement is designed to save tax dollars and, at the same time, to achieve the goal of public assistance—providing basic living expenses to the destitute. To implement it would be to repay a debt to ourselves and to the victims of poverty.

CHAPTER 11

Paying the Piper

It is one of the many problems besetting welfare reform that its proponents have become true believers of two contending creeds.

One has held that only a broad, "comprehensive" reform would meet the national need. The other has sought to achieve "incremental" reform, on a step-by-step basis. Although they agree on the necessity of reforming the welfare mess, the two sides have been at odds about appropriate tactics, and great friction has as a result developed between them.

The only significant rewards of the dispute have been rhetorical. Rare heights have been achieved by some contending stylists. I know. I have been an active participant for fifteen years.

Meantime, no progress has been made toward achieving welfare reform.

Political reality—the way votes line up in Congress—clearly indicates there will be no full-scale, comprehensive reform in the next few years. Limited advance may, however, be possible.

My hope, then, is that we can move ahead at the practicable pace. I would only insist that in proceeding incrementally we be certain we are moving toward the accomplishment of the all-ecompassing system that the nation has so long needed.

Putting a Lid on Welfare Spending: The Role of Substitution

The Graduated Income Supplement that I urge can be designed to eliminate the need for any increased spending to introduce work incentives. The $298 billion in current official spending on income transfer programs is adequate for financing a new system. Any additional costs under the Graduated Income Supplement would be offset by the considerable savings that could be realized from the elimination of the welfare bureaucracy and the agencies concerned with making a host of other payments. Almost from the outset, the cost of benefits should also be cut thanks to the operation of the work incentive.

Indeed, the net budget cost of implementing the Graduated Income Supplement can be kept to zero. This cannot be done in the style of President Carter's successive "welfare reform" proposals, by simply dealing with those programs popularly known as welfare. If income transfer programs are understood to include *all of those which provide any form of income supplementation or replacement,* the savings that can be realized by adopting the Graduated Income Supplement in their place should be sufficient to cover possible added costs. In short, all new or increased assistance can be funded from the budgets of programs which should no longer be necessary or justified.

Full-scale implementation of the Graduated Income

Supplement could be accomplished with the stipulation that no additional dollars should be spent on income transfer programs. By encompassing all existing programs in this reform, we would give it adequate funding to make it self-financing, thus removing a major obstacle to its success. Existing federal, state, and local income transfers were valued at approximately $298 billion in 1977, as we have seen. Their termination would generate enough revenues to give every American about $1,355. For a family of four, this payment would amount to an annual income of $5,420—just short of the 1977 poverty line of $5,850. Even if such a payment were made subject to income taxes, the net benefit to most recipients would be as high as their current payments under existing income transfer programs.

To be sure, immediate substitution of the Graduated Income Supplement for all existing income transfer programs is not politically feasible. For one thing, existing programs are woven deeply into the social and economic fabric of our nation. Almost all of these programs have been designed to meet specific needs, and each of these needs has its own constituency. Such groups will be reluctant to see the dissolution of programs on which they have become dependent until they can be convinced of the superiority of comprehensive reform.

Although the total replacement of existing income-transfer programs by the Graduated Income Supplement is a desirable goal, the immediate objective must certainly be more limited. Yet, in whatever steps we take, we must keep in mind that the essence of successful self-financing welfare reform is the concept of substitution. The replacement of current programs rather than the addition of new programs must be the hallmark of any reform if it is to succeed.

Preliminary research has been conducted by The Institute for Socioeconomic Studies into the substitution effect for various levels of grants. One plan for substitution would eliminate a specific transfer program and distribute the revenues involved to all recipients of the Graduated Income Supplement. Another approach would assure current recipients of the same dollar amount of payments, but through the Graduated Income Supplement mechanism rather than through categorical programs.

Preliminary estimates indicate the extent to which the GIS would be self-financing. For example, a GIS grant of $1,000 per person would generate revenues from taxes and the effects of cashing out in-kind support which would cover 67 percent of its cost. The self-financing character of the GIS would be enhanced if the payment were lower. A GIS of $600 per person would provide 80 percent of its own cost. By contrast, a benefit of $2,000 per person would be 56 percent self-supporting.

CHAPTER 12

The First Step

A New Incremental Approach

Both Nixon's FAP and Carter's PBJI were defeated by an ad hoc coalition. Some of its members claimed that the proposals were too sweeping. Others insisted that they did not go far enough. The essence of the conflict is the mistrust between the partisans of incremental reform of welfare and those of comprehensive reform.

Political analysts have taught that democracy prefers to undertake reform in incremental steps, except in times of emergency. Our political process is based on compromise and gradualism. David Braybrooke, a philosopher, and Charles E. Lindblom, an economist, have described the process.

For a democracy like the United States, they maintain, the commitment to incremental change is not surprising. Nonincremental alternatives usually do not lie within the range of choices possible in the society or body politic. Societies, it goes without saying, are complex structures that can avoid dissolution only by meeting certain preconditions, among them the one that certain kinds of change are admissible only if they occur slowly. Political democracy is often greatly endangered by nonincremental change, which it can accommodate only in certain limited circumstances.

To pursue incremental changes is to direct policy toward comprehensive reform; it is also to pursue long-term changes through a sequence of moves. Avoiding cleavage along social lines, which is exacerbated when issues of ultimate principle are raised, incremental politics explores a continuing series of remedial moves on which some agreement can be developed even among members of opposing ideological camps.

It can be argued, of course, that proposals for comprehensive welfare reform, including the Graduated Income Supplement, do not represent the kind of comprehensive change to which Braybrooke and Lindblom refer. The great social change was actually accomplished in 1935, when the United States—breaking with its long history of relying on voluntary and informal action to aid the poor—began a program of formal government relief. Comprehensive change would amount to no more than a reform of that fundamental decision.

Principles for an Incremental Approach

Adherence to the following principles will be necessary as we proceed incrementally toward comprehensive reform:

1. Programs must be consolidated to achieve administrative simplicity and integration of benefits.
2. Cash programs are to be preferred over in-kind programs.

3. Cash benefits must be taxable to help recoup payments from recipients who are not needy.
4. The net cost in the federal budget must be zero; income supplementation must be funded by substitution for existing programs, by tax recoupment, and by savings generated by increased efficiency.

Other factors must also be considered in redesigning the nation's public assistance program. For example, the cost of administrative decentralization must be realistically estimated. All too often, in doling out welfare benefits, state and local governments have given way to political pressures from the groups demanding benefit increases. Moreover, rather than providing a useful degree of local control, welfare at the state and local level has spawned extensive duplication of benefits and programs and an overblown welfare bureaucracy.

While it is true that federal administration is more remote from recipients than are local authorities, this situation has its advantages. Administrators may be somewhat insulated from at least the most direct forms of pressure—sit-ins, picketing, and other demonstrations—which tend to cause an escalation of benefits rather than a prudent policy.

Discrepancies in benefits among states, variations in the cost of living notwithstanding, are inequitable and self-defeating. In fact, they cause one of the most serious problems in the current system—welfare migration. No matter what their ideological perspective, most analysts now recognize that disparities in welfare benefits have caused a substantial population movement from low-benefit states, such as those in the South, to the high-benefit states of the North and West. The influx of welfare recipients has imposed a heavy burden on many states and has been a major contributor to the financial woes of some of our largest cities.

In a modest way, the federal government has already begun to reduce the differences among states. Recent reforms have included incentives for states to raise their benefits, which is particularly important for low-benefit states. More important, the Food Stamp program has served to raise the level of the public assistance in low-benefit states closer to the poverty level. This program is in itself the forerunner of a national minimum-benefit approach.

Introducing the Graduated Income Supplement by Increments

The Graduated Income Supplement could be introduced and funded by making all existing income transfer benefits taxable. Because of exemptions, no tax is payable by a family whose income is below the poverty line. Making benefits taxable would thus not come at the expense of the poor. Research conducted by The Institute for Socioeconomic Studies shows that taxing benefits in 1977 would yield about $25 billion in revenue. We could use this revenue for initiating the GIS.

When the GIS is implemented, existing benefits will be replaced dollar for dollar by the cashing-out process. If the level of the new supplement were one hundred dollars per person, that hundred dollars would be deducted from the checks sent to each beneficiary of any federally funded program. A substantial portion of the cost of the GIS would be recovered through this cashout process. The portion not recovered by cashout would be funded by the benefits tax.

Among the numerous advantages of this approach is a smoothing of notches in existing programs. The GIS would be payable to all regardless of income. Beneficiaries could go to work without fear of the abrupt loss of transfer income. There would be a better targeting of benefits under this system, since much of the cash paid to the non-poor would be recouped by taxes, leaving more funds available for needy families. Those who worry that additional spending would be an inevitable concomitant of welfare reform should thus be reassured: the Graduated Income Supplement would not involve a single cent of additional spending by the federal government.

Once this reform was accomplished, we could move to the second stage. Using the substitution techniques suggested earlier, we could begin to consolidate the welter of existing welfare and income-support programs. As programs were combined or eliminated, the resulting savings could be used to increase the level of the Graduated Income Supplement. The availability of advanced computer technology would simplify this process.

Early candidates for consolidation and cashing out would be AFDC and food stamps. At first, the cash value of the food stamps could be added to AFDC payments for those who receive both. For others, food stamps would simply be replaced by cash payments. Food Stamp benefits might also be consolidated with SSI payments. Eventually, with the guarantee that no welfare recipient would suffer a loss in benefits, the new single welfare payment could be folded into the Graduated Income Supplement.

This process, like others that affect income-support programs, could actually result in major savings in administrative costs. The Food Stamp program would almost certainly be moved out of the Agriculture Department and into the Department of Health and Human Services, which is responsible for welfare administration.

As this folding in of income support programs progressed, the Graduated Income Supplement would develop to the point where it could meet the basic living expenses of the poor. At that point, it would no longer be necessary to have a distinct welfare program at all.

The incremental approach could thus be used to introduce the Graduated Income Supplement, each step progressing toward the ultimate substitution of the supplement for all current income-support programs.

We have probably all heard some version of this criticism of the current welfare program: "If we took all the money we waste on welfare and just gave it to the public, with no strings attached, there wouldn't be any more poor people."

Although it grows out of the enormous feelings of frustration that are experienced by both contributors and recipients, the above sentiment contains the basic concept of the necessary reform. It is a common-sense reaction to a myriad of programs that no longer correspond to the needs of our society.

We should never lose sight of the most significant advantage to be gained from the introduction of the Graduated Income Supplement in place of other income-support programs—it will remove the distinction between the free enterprise economy and the dependency economy!

All people would be eligible for the same program. It would have a strong work incentive. Everyone would be protected against destitution. Others would receive varying degrees of tax relief, which would diminish as income rose.

Not only the welfare mess, but welfare itself would be ended.

Summary

America is in troubled times. The deterioration of free enterprise and opportunity have reduced our once exalted position in the world economy to that of an inefficient, losing competitor. But I strongly believe that this trend can be reversed.

The key is welfare reform. It must be accomplished in a manner that does not deny free enterprise. To be sure, our economic system does not bring prosperity to all. Some do not successfully play the game. While admitting that, we must also recognize that there is ample room to eliminate poverty without killing free enterprise in the process.

I have confidence in America—in its ability to produce the goods that the world demands, and in its ability to alleviate the suffering of its poor citizens. My program combines these two articles of faith by giving the poor the incentive to join the system so that prosperity can be shared by all.

Appendix

An Analysis of
a Taxable Demogrant

I. Introduction

This section presents the methodology and basic results of the "substitution analysis" carried out at The Institute for Socioeconomic Studies. The purpose of the substitution project has been to explore the fiscal impact of substituting a demogrant, i.e., a non-income-tested transfer based solely on demographic criteria, such as age, for all or part of the existing transfer system.

The system we wish to explore is one in which the demogrant would be paid out universally on an individual (as opposed to family) basis. This demogrant would be taxable, so individuals facing low marginal tax rates would keep a large fraction of their demogrant payment, whereas those facing high marginal tax rates would return a large fraction of it in taxes. The use of the existing tax system would thus inject an element of progressivity or implicit income testing into the demogrant.

The system we envision would substitute for or "cash out" existing benefit payments in such a way that no individual would be left worse off as a result of the change in the transfer policy. (Some individuals, however, would be left worse off as a result of the change in the tax policy, i.e., as a result of moving to a system of taxable benefits.) Individuals currently receiving less than the designated demogrant would simply receive the demogrant under the new system; i.e., they would be made better off by an amount equal to the difference between the demogrant and current payments. Those currently receiving more than the designated demogrant would continue to receive the same amount under the new system; i.e., they would receive the demogrant plus the excess of their current payments over the demogrant. Thus the transfer payment to any given individual would, in our demogrant system, equal the designated demogrant or the amount of the benefits received from the current system, whichever was larger.

The rationale for applying such a "no losers" substitution policy is simply that it is difficult to seriously imagine an immediate, complete replacement of the existing transfer system. The latter has developed powerful political constituencies and has created patterns of dependency that cannot be eliminated overnight. The "no losers" policy that we envision should thus be seen as a realistic first step toward a true replacement of the current patchwork system. Movement toward a complete elimination of this system could be achieved by the use of a "grandfather clause" under which current recipients would retain their present benefits. However, these recipients would be dropped from existing programs when they ceased to be eligible, and no new participants would be enrolled. In the long run a complete cashout could thus be effected.

In order to analyze the fiscal impact of a taxable demogrant, we must calculate two types of recoupment. First we need to estimate the amount of the currently paid benefits that would be cashed out by the demogrant. From a long perspective (that is, if we were to imagine a complete replacement of the current system), the annual recoupment from a cashout would simply equal the total dollar amount of the benefits currently being disbursed. However, the "no losers" constraint we have chosen to impose on the cashout complicates the calculations considerably. In particular, we need to determine, for any demogrant amount, what fraction of the population is receiving less than that amount in current benefits and what fraction of the total benefits accrues to that part of the population. The latter information is not available in any systematic fashion; in order to calculate the recoupment via reductions in benefit payments for the type of demogrant we are analyzing, we have therefore had to estimate the distribution function of benefits across the population.

The second recoupment that must be estimated is the increase in tax receipts that would result from the substitution of a taxable demogrant for existing, nontaxable benefits. The increase in each individual's tax base equals the amount of the demogrant, and since the demogrant is universal, the computation of the tax recoupment is reasonably straightforward. We need to know the distribution of marginal tax rates by income brackets and the changes in tax brackets that would result from the addition of the demogrant to taxable income, and this information is available (with some adjustments) from government publications.

The task of analyzing the fiscal impact of a taxable demogrant thus breaks down into several steps. First, we need to estimate the distribution function of benefits across the population and to use this estimated distribution to calculate the recoupment from a cashout. The methods used to perform this estimation are the subject of the next section of the Appendix. Second, we need to compute the tax recoupment, and this problem is considered in the third section. Third, we need to compare the sum of recoupments from the cashout and increased tax receipts with the total of demogrant payments from various demogrant levels in order to estimate the fiscal impact of a taxable demogrant. The fourth section performs this comparison under a variety of assumptions and summarizes our results. Finally, some conclusions and suggested extensions are offered in the last section.

2. Methodology for Estimating the Distribution of Transfer Payments

The most difficult data requirement from the substitution analysis is the estimation of the distribution function of transfer benefits across the population. What fraction of the population receives $1,000 or less, what fraction receives $2,000 or less, and so on? The benefit distribution is difficult to determine because of the problem of benefit overlap. Although we have a reasonable idea of how many individuals participate in any given program and therefore have a good idea of the average benefits paid out under each, we lack reliable information about the number of individuals who simultaneously benefit from two or more programs.

One possible way to develop information about benefit overlap would be to examine the rich bodies of microdata that exist, e.g., the Michigan Income Dynamics data or those from the MATCH model. In practice, however, no individual data set has a sufficient coverage of program overlaps to satisfy our requirements, and a meaningful merger of the results from these microdata sets is precluded by the special nature of each. As an alternative, we have chosen a more macro or aggregate approach. Beginning with published data on the number of participants and the total benefits paid in federally initiated programs, we use a procedure of "selective aggregation" together with an "independence assumption" to generate the hypothesized distribution of benefits across the population.

Since so little is known about benefit overlap, the procedure to be explained in this section is potentially both interesting and useful, quite apart from its connection with demogrants. The question of benefit incidence is of interest in and of itself. Although the reader may differ with the specifics of our procedure, it is hoped that our exercise will at least provide a benchmark for use in assessing the benefits distribution.

To initiate our procedure it is useful to begin with a hypothetical example. Consider a world with two transfer programs, A and B. For any individual there are four participation possibilities—participation in neither program, in A alone, in B alone, or in both A and B. If we know the fractions of the population participating in A and in B (equal to p_A and p_B, say) and *if we assume that participation in A is independent of participation in B,* then we can compute the probability of joint participation in A and B as the product of the marginal participation probabilities, i.e., as $p_A p_B$. Likewise, we can compute the probability of each of three other participation possibilities. *If we also assume that all participants in any given program receive the same benefit from the program,* then we have enough information to construct a benefits distribution.

Suppose, for example, that 20 percent of the population participates in A and that an average benefit of $2,000 is received from that program, while 70 percent of the population participates in B with an average benefit of $1,000. Then according to our assumptions, 25 percent of the population receives no benefit ($0.24 = [1 - 1.2][1 - 0.7]$, 56 percent receives a benefit of $1,000, 6 percent receives a benefit of $2,000, and 14 percent receives a benefit of $3,000.

This procedure is not limited to the hypothetical two-program example. So long as we are willing to retain the assumptions of mutual independence of participation in the various programs and of equal benefits for all participants from any given program, the procedure suggested above can be extended to any number of programs.

Unfortunately, the two assumptions underlying these computations are clearly false. A person who benefits from AFDC is more likely to benefit from Food Stamps than is a randomly chosen member of the population, i.e., participations in the two programs are not independent. Indeed, there are several major programs that are either mutually inclusive or mutually exclusive, e.g., everyone eligible for AFDC is also eligible for Medicaid. (The converse, however, is not true.) Furthermore, benefits from many transfer programs are income conditioned; for example, the assumption that all food stamp recipients garner equal benefits is seriously incorrect.

Retaining the simplicity of our approach while at the same time making our assumptions more tolerable approximations to reality requires some manipulations. Our first step is to classify each individual into one of six mutually exclusive age-income groups. Each individual is either poor (i.e., belongs to a family with income below the poverty line) or is nonpoor, and each individual is a child (under eighteen), is an adult (eighteen to sixty-two), or is elderly. The distribution of the U.S. population across these six cells as of 1977 is given in Table 1. This particular two-by-three classification was chosen as the minimum categorization needed to ensure a reasonable degree of homogeneity within each subgroup of the population. That is, this subdivision represents an attempt to make the assumptions of equal probabilities of participation in the various programs and of equal dollar transfers for participants in any given program reasonable within each cell. Thus, while it is clearly not reasonable to assume that a poor adult and a nonpoor child have the same probability of participating in Food Stamps, it is not too unreasonable to assign the same participation probability to all poor children. Nor does it seem too unreasonable to assume, for the purpose of estimating the benefits distribution, that all poor children participating in Food Stamps receive approximately the same annual benefit from that program. Of course, greater homogeneity within cells could be achieved by a finer subdivision of the population, but the data on program-participation rates and benefit receipts that would be needed are not available.

The second step is to aggregate programs in such a way as to make the "independence assumption" as plausible as possible. The principle underlying the aggregation is to group together those programs that are either mutually exclusive or mutually inclusive within each age-income cell. For example, participation in a veterans' program related to service disabilities is assumed to preclude participation in a similar program relating to nonservice disabilities. In order to avoid a flagrant violation of the independence assumption, we therefore place all such disability programs into a common veterans category. Similarly, since all Medicare recipients are also Social Security beneficiaries and since all Social Security beneficiaries are eligible for Medicare, separate categories for the two programs would violate the independence assumption. Accordingly, the two programs are grouped together in a common retirement category. (The fact that the nonelderly do not receive retirement benefits causes no problems. We simply set the probability of participation in retirement equal to zero for children and adults.)

This aggregation procedure seems to generate reasonable results for most programs, but there is one type of interaction among programs that requires special treatment. Suppose the set of participants in one program, say program A, forms a proper subset of the set of participants in another program, say program B. That is, suppose all of the participants in A also benefit from B but not all of the beneficiaries of B participate in A. If A and B are aggregated, the assumption that all beneficiaries of the aggregate program receive equal benefits is violated; but if A and B are kept separate, then the independence assumption is violated.

The solution to this dilemma lies in the recognition that our two key assumptions need hold only within each population cell (as opposed to across cells) for our procedure to be valid. Suppose A is a proper subset of B in some cell. We can split the population of that cell into two subcells, those who participate in both A and B and those who do not participate in A, and define the combination of A with B as one program, and B without A as a second program. Then in the first subcell the probability of participation in the combined program is set equal to one, and the probability of participation in B alone is set equal to zero; similarly, in the second subcell the probability of participation in the combined program is set equal to zero, and the probability of participation in B alone is set equal to the conditional probability of participation in B, given nonparticipation in A. Within each of the subcells, both of the key assumptions once again become valid.

Once all the transfer programs have been aggregated and allocated to cells in such a way that the independence assumption and the assumption that all participants in a given program receive the same benefit from that program are tenable within each cell, computing the benefits distribution becomes straightforward. In any given cell, each aggregate transfer program is assigned a marginal participation probability and an average-benefit level. The benefits distribution within that cell is then derived by matching the number of participants in each possible program combination (as the product of the number of individuals in the cell and the joint participation probabilities) with the sum of average benefits for the programs in that combination. Since each individual falls into one, and only one, population cell, the distribution of benefits for the population as a whole is simply obtained by ordering the distributions within each cell and then merging the intracell distributions.

The above explains our methodology for estimating the distribution function of benefits. This methodology is a general one in the sense that it can be applied using various definitions of "benefit." Such generality is, of course, desirable since several difficult issues are involved in defining exactly what one means by a benefit or transfer payment. There are, for example, the problems of what monetary value to impute to in-kind transfers, or how to draw the line between transfer payments and deferred compensation, and of how to treat programs which are in part self-financing. Furthermore, there are questions of how to treat state and local transfer payments—whether they should be included at all, whether only those expenditures mandated by federal programs should be included, and so forth.

Since there is no obviously "correct" definition of "benefit," we have used three different ones in our estimations of the benefits distribution, and our analysis could be extended by using other definitional bases. Our basic analysis, i.e., our benchmark definition, uses research previously carried out through The Institute, namely, W. Lawrence and S. Leeds, *An Inventory of Federal Income Transfer Programs: Fiscal Year 1977* (The Institute for Socioeconomic Studies, 1978). The *Federal Inventory* by Lawrence and Leeds lists $248 billion in transfer payments for the fiscal year 1977 and includes all public transfer programs that provide benefits to individuals in the forms of direct or indirect cash benefits, of in-kind benefits, and of credit or insurance benefits. Transfer payments whose overriding aim is to influence economic behavior, rather than to provide income support and expenditures on public goods, are not included in the $248 billion total. (See pp. 4–5 in the *Federal Inventory*.) Many of the programs included in the *Federal Inventory* are "transfer payments" only by virtue of a very broad definition, but most observers would agree to calling a large percentage of the *expenditure* transfer payments. In any event, the *Federal Inventory* serves as a good starting point for the analysis.

Of course, the data in the *Federal Inventory* cannot be directly loaded into our model. It is necessary to aggregate programs and to expand the list of population cells so that the essential assumptions underlying the analysis can be used. In addition, it is necessary to use federal data sources in order to go beyond the information in the *Federal Inventory* on numbers of participants and expenditures across the population cells. A considerable amount of effort has been expended on collecting and organizing the data so as to make it compatible with the model's format.

There are twenty-eight transfer programs listed in the *Federal Inventory* with expenditures of greater than $1 billion for the fiscal year 1977, and we have aggregated these into eleven major program categories. These twenty-eight programs account for 77 percent of the total expenditures of $248 billion. In addition, we have added a twelfth residual category encompassing all programs paying out less than $1 billion in that year. The aggregation procedure has been reasonably straightforward, but the interrelationship between Medicaid, AFDC, SSI, and unemployment insurance needs some comment. To a first approximation, AFDC and SSI are mutually exclusive among poor adults, and participants in these two programs form a proper subset of the poor adult Medicaid population. In addition, Medicaid and UI are approximately mutually exclusive but differ substantially in average benefits and as a result cannot be reasonably aggregated. In accordance with our general methodology, we have therefore split the adult-poor population into four subcells: adult-poor (AFDC + Medicaid), adult-poor (SSI + Medicaid), adult-poor (unemployment insurance), and adult-poor (Medicaid residual). Likewise the child-poor cell has been split into an AFDC +

Medicaid subcell and a Medicaid residual subcell, and the elderly-poor cell has been split into an SSI + Medicaid subcell and a Medicaid residual subcell. Our model thus operates on eleven population cells, the three nonpoor cells and the eight subcells.

Summaries of the assumptions underlying the aggregation procedure and of the results of that aggregation are presented in Tables 2 and 3. Table 2 gives an overview of how the twelve program categories were constructed, while Table 3 presents the data used in the computation of the benefits distribution, i.e., average benefit levels and marginal participation probabilities for each of the twelve program categories across each of the eleven cells. Discussion of the estimation results and of the sensitivity of those results to variations in the definition of benefit is deferred to section 4.

3. Estimation of the Tax Recoupment

The tax recoupment associated with a demogrant may be considered independently of the benefits distribution and of the recoupment from a cashout, since while the demogrant is assumed to be taxable, the benefits to be cashed out are not. If existing transfer payments were taxable, then to compute the tax recoupment one would need to know how the increment in taxable income due to the difference between predemogrant and postdemogrant transfers varied with income across the population; that is, one would need to know the joint distribution of income and benefits. However, since existing benefits are not taxable, the increment in each individual's taxable income is simply the level of the demogrant.

An important implication of the separability of the cashout recoupment from the tax recoupment is that it is possible to consistently treat the former on an *individual* basis while at the same time treating the latter on a *family* or household basis. That is, of course, essential, since the income tax is applied to family income in the U.S.

The estimation of the tax recoupment is straightforward. First, the impact of the demogrant on the distribution of family income is computed; then the existing schedule of marginal tax rates is applied to the implied increment in taxable income. The distribution of family income is approximated by using published data on the distribution of families by income level, and a schedule of marginal rates is derived by associating an average family size with each income bracket. The impact of a demogrant is to shift a fraction of the families within each bracket into the next highest bracket.

It is assumed that the distribution of income within each income bracket is uniform; i.e., we approximate the density function of income by a step function. This intrabracket distributional assumption (or, indeed, any other assumption about how income is distributed within each income bracket) makes the computation of the effect of a demogrant on the distribution of taxable family income easy, since the demogrant's effect is simply to shift the step function to the right by the amount of the demogrant. (However, a special feature must be introduced to deal with families receiving zero taxable income before the demogrant. This "tax exemption" feature of the model restricts the fraction of families in the zero income bracket who are shifted to the next highest level.) The highest income bracket will gain families as a result of the demogrant, the zero income bracket will lose families, and the intermediate brackets may either gain or lose families, depending on whether the number of families upgraded into the bracket exceeds the number of those upgraded out of it.

Once the new distribution of families by income bracket has been estimated, the assumption of a uniform intrabracket distribution is reimposed, and the change in taxable income due to the demogrant for each bracket can be computed as the product of average income for the income bracket and the change in the number of families within the cell.

The result of this computation is a vector which has as many elements as there are income brackets, each element registering the corresponding aggregate changes in taxable incomes. The tax recoupment from any cell is simply the product of the marginal tax rate and the change in taxable income for the cell; then, the total tax recoupment is simply the sum over the tax recoupments for all of the income brackets. The estimation of the tax recoupment is incorporated into the results presented in the next section.

4. Summary of Results

This section summarizes the results of the substitution analysis and examines the sensitivity of those results with respect to the definition of benefit that we used for the analysis. We begin by presenting an estimate of the benefits distribution, using our benchmark definition of transfer payment, i.e., the one based on the *Federal Inventory*. This benefits distribution is used to estimate the cashout that derives from reductions in benefit payments associated with various levels of the demogrant. The recoupment from the benefit cashout is then added to the revenues generated by the taxes levied on the demogrant, i.e., the tax recoupment, to produce an estimate of the total recoupment or *gross cashout* associated with the demogrant levels. Finally, in order to compute the total fiscal impact or *excess burden* of various levels of the demogrant, we compare total demogrant payments (equal to the level of the demogrant times the number of individuals in the population) to the gross cashout.

To examine the sensitivity of our results we investigate the effects of making two major changes in the definition of benefit. This first change is to eliminate certain of the *Federal Inventory* programs from the benefits base—in particular, those programs which could be regarded as primarily providing deferred compensation and those which are essentially self-financing. (This first definitional change requires a new aggregation procedure, i.e., our programs need to be grouped in a different fashion, so we refer to this alternative definitional base as the "regrouping.") Of course, this definitional change reduces the number of programs subject to cashout and therefore worsens the fiscal impact of the taxable demogrant. The real question is whether this rather significant definitional change induces a significant change in fiscal impact. The second definitional change we make is to add state and local expenditures onto federally mandated programs, using the regrouped program cluster as a base. The combined effect of regrouping and inclusion of state and local expenditures is to decrease slightly total benefit payments relative to the benchmark definition but to change significantly the composition of that total. Again, the objective is to explore the sensitivity of the analysis to changes in the definitional base.

We can begin by examining the estimated benefits distribution based on our benchmark definition of transfer payment. Figure 1 presents the cumulative-distribution function of benefits across the population; i.e., benefit levels are graphed on the horizontal axis, and the fraction of the population receiving no more than each benefit level is graphed on the vertical axis. For example, the first point on our estimated distribution function indicates that approximately 58 percent of the population (about 123 million individuals) receives no more than $292 annually in transfer payments. (This point is derived from our estimate of an average residual-category benefit of $292 per year, paid to the 123 million nonpoor children, adults, and elderly not receiving any other benefits.)

Our estimates indicate that approximately two-thirds of the population receives a rather low level of annual benefits ($400 or less per year). Between the 70th and 90th percentiles there is a steady progression from the $400 a-year level up to the $4,000-a-year level. This range corresponds to those individuals who benefit from one or more programs that pay out relatively modest amounts. Just short of the 90th percentile (at 187 million "cumulative persons") there is a "bulge" in the distribution, representing the approximately 15 million individuals assumed to receive the full Social Security average retirement benefit, and thereafter one can see the relatively small fraction of the population that receives quite large annual transfer payments. This last group represents mainly those who benefit from one or more programs in addition to receiving full Social Security benefits.

The estimated distribution function of benefits is directly related to the recoupment that could be obtained by cashing out benefits according to the "no losers" substitution constraint. The per capita benefits cashout for any demogrant level is given by that demogrant level less the integral under the benefits distribution function up to that level.* Note the implication that the nature of the benefits-distribution function for benefit levels higher than the demogrant being considered is irrelevant. This is obvious, on reflection, since the cashout from an individual who receives benefits in an amount greater than the demogrant simply equals the demogrant itself. Whether the individual is receiving considerably more or only a bit more in benefits than the demogrant level has no bearing on the recoupment from the benefits cashout.

To assess the fiscal significance of the benefits cashout we examine how the ratio of benefit recoupment to demogrant payments varies with the level of the demogrant. This *cashout ratio* is presented in Figure 2, and it simply tells us what fraction of the demogrant payments could be financed out of recouped benefits. The cashout ratio declines as the demogrant increases, because the fraction of the population from which the full demogrant can be recovered decreases as the demogrant rises; that is, the numerator of the cashout ratio necessarily increases at a slower rate than the denominator does.

Since a large fraction of the population is receiving relatively low levels of transfer payments, the cashout ratio declines quite

---

*Let $F(b)$ denote the distribution function of b, and let $f(b)$ denote the associated density function. For a demogrant level of d, the per capita benefits cashout may be computed as

$$c = \int_0^\infty \min[b,d]f(b)db$$
$$= \int_0^d bf(b)db + [1 - F(d)]d$$
$$= d - \int_0^d F(b)db.$$

rapidly with increases in the demogrant. For example, at a demo-grant level of one thousand dollars per year, only slightly more than 50 percent of the demogrant payments are covered by re-ductions in benefit payments. However, in order to complete the account of the fiscal impact of the taxable demogrant, one must also add in the revenues generated from the tax recoupment.

The ratio of total recoupment, i.e., benefits recoupment plus tax recoupment, to demogrant payments is presented in Figure 3 as the *gross cashout ratio*. The ratio of tax recoupment to demo-grant payments is in the range of 20–25 percent and increases slightly with increases in the demogrant, since at higher levels of the demogrant individuals are paying taxes on that transfer at higher marginal tax rates. As a result, the gross cashout ratio declines much less rapidly than does the simple cashout ratio net of the tax recoupment. For example, at the demogrant level of $1,000 per year, the combined recoupment from benefits plus taxes covers almost 75 percent of demogrant payments. The tax recoupment thus constitutes a significant part of the potential financing for a demogrant.

The gross cashout ratio can be used to assess the "cost" or excess burden of the taxable demogrant, if by cost one means the additional taxes that would be required above and beyond the recoupments. For example, at a demogrant level of approxi-mately $425 per year the gross cashout ratio equals one; i.e., the excess burden of the demogrant is zero, since total recoupments just cover total demogrant payments. (Remember that the demo-grant is to be awarded on an individual basis, so that a demogrant of $425 per year represents an annual payment of $1,700 for a family of four.) Likewise, at other demogrant levels we can com-pute the associated excess burden as the level of the demogrant times one minus the gross cashout ratio.

However, a more revealing way to present the "cost" of a taxable demogrant is to focus on the average change in individual tax payments that would be required to completely cover the cost of the demogrant, i.e., to focus on the *per capita excess burden*. This per capita excess burden is presented in Figure 4 as a function of the demogrant, and it ranges from an average tax rebate of $62 per person per year for a $292-per-year demogrant up to an average tax increase of $262 per year for a demogrant of $1,000 and beyond.

These excess-burden figures provide the final assessment of the fiscal impact of a taxable demogrant. Whether one considers an average tax increase of $262 per year above and beyond benefit and tax recoupments to be too large a cost to bear to finance a demogrant of $1,000 per year is a matter of personal taste, since what this $262-per-year figure (or whatever the excess burden happens to be) really represents is some hint of the redistribution involved in a demogrant. Or perhaps more directly, the excess-burden figures measure the per capita change in personal finance that would flow into and then back out of the government tax system.

We can now examine the sensitivity of the analysis to changes in the definitional base. The two changes we consider are (1) a narrowing of the benefits base through "regrouping" and (2) changes in the composition of the base via the addition of state and local expenditures on federally mandated programs to the regrouped program aggregates. The basic assumptions underlying these new definitions are given in Tables 4 and 5, and the resulting input data, i.e., marginal participation probabilities and average benefit levels, are presented in Tables 6 and 7.

The effects of these redefinitions on the estimated distribution of benefits and on the associated calculation of the fiscal impact of the taxable demogrant can be seen in Tables 8–10. Table 8 presents the three cumulative-distribution functions, Table 9 presents the three gross cashout ratios as functions of the demogrant, and Table 10 presents the three per capita excess burdens as functions of the demogrant.

The effect of "regrouping" is to shift the cumulative-distribution function of benefits to the left relative to the benchmark distribution; that is, at any benefit level the fraction of the population receiving an annual transfer of no more than that amount increases relative to the benchmark case. Adding state and local expenditures on federally mandated programs onto the regrouped program base induces some changes in the form of the distribution function relative to the benchmark distribution without bringing about any overall shift.

The conclusion of this exercise appears to be that these changes in the definition of benefit have relatively minor effects on the fiscal feasibility of a taxable demogrant. Although these changes do affect the gross cashout ratios and the per capita excess burdens, the changes in these fiscal measures are not as large as one might have expected. For example, at a demogrant level of $600 per year the use of the regrouped program base as opposed to the benchmark base implies an increase in the per capita excess burden of less than $23 per year. The third definition, i.e., the addition of state and local expenditures to the regrouped base, has almost no fiscal effect.

There are two reasons why the fiscal impact of the taxable demogrant is not very sensitive to change in the definition of benefit. The first is simply that the definitional changes we have made, and indeed any changes that one might reasonably make, are inconsequential relative to the great bulk of transfer payments. The second is that many of the definitional questions that one might raise affect the upper range of the benefits distribution, and changes in this range are irrelevant from a fiscal point of view. Thus, while one might object to the transfer-payment base used in our basic model, from a practical point of view this definition does not make much of a difference. Those programs that most observers would agree to call "transfer payments" seem to generate the basic results of the model.

5. Conclusion

The preceding analysis goes some distance toward suggesting the fiscal feasibility of a taxable demogrant. We find that an individual demogrant of $425 per year, i.e., an annual demogrant of $1,700 for a family of four, is affordable in the sense that this level of demogrant could be completely financed out of benefit and tax recoupments. This conclusion is based on our estimate of the cumulative distribution function of benefits across the population and appears to be robust with respect to changes in the definition of benefit used. Although such definitional changes have some impact on the estimated distribution of benefits, these changes tend to be concentrated in the upper range of that distribution and therefore do not affect our fiscal conclusions.

Of course, this analysis is far from complete, in the sense that it could be extended in several directions. One of the possible extensions that has been discussed is an investigation of a differentiated demogrant, e.g., a demogrant that would transfer different amounts to different age groups. The analysis could also be improved by further estimations based on alternative definitional bases, including different aggregation procedures. For example, the possibility of disaggregating the Social Security program into several subprograms according to the level of benefit paid has been discussed. More exotic extensions that have also been considered include questions of how to model the dynamics of a movement from a "no losers" substitution to a complete cashout that would eliminate all transfers other than the demogrant and how to merge the tax and cashout analyses to explicitly examine the redistribution aspects of the demogrant.

However, these extensions go beyond our original objective, which was simply to investigate the fiscal feasibility of the taxable demogrant. The results presented here definitely suggest such feasibility.

TABLE 1

DISTRIBUTION OF U.S. POPULATION
(in thousands)

	CHILD UNDER 18	ADULT 18–62	ELDERLY OVER 62	TOTAL
Poor	10,273	10,807	3,895	24,975
Nonpoor	53,592	109,966	23,770	187,328
TOTAL	63,865	120,773	27,665	212,303

TABLE 2

CONSTRUCTION OF THE 12 PROGRAM CATEGORIES

(Expenditures in millions, Participants in thousands)

PROGRAM	EXPENDITURE	PARTICIPANTS	COMMENTS
A. Food Stamps	$ 5,474	30,000	
B. School Lunch	2,204	27,000	
C. Veterans (excl. survivors)	13,211	6,500	Disability programs assumed mutually exclusive. Some overlap of disability with education and hospitalization assumed.
Hospitalization	2,862	1,210	
Service Disability	4,796	2,860	
Education	3,683	2,000	
Nonservice Disability	1,870	1,880	
D. Survivors	23,508	10,385	Survivor programs assumed mutually exclusive.
Civil Service	1,205	400	
Railroad	1,026	400	
Social Security	18,888	7,500	

Program			Note
Veteran Service Death	1,067	475	
Veteran Pension	1,322	1,610	
E. Disability	13,319	4,800	Disability programs assumed mutually exclusive.
Civil Service	1,694	300	
Social Security	11,625	4,500	
F. BEOGs	1,461	2,000	
G. AFDC+Medicaid	11,100	13,247	All programs are mutually inclusive.
AFDC	5,718		
Social Services	2,645		
Housing	1,112		
Medicaid to AFDCRecipients	1,635		
H. Medicaid Residual	3,896	5,902	Recipients of Medicaid who receive neither AFDC nor SSI.
I. Retirement	90,161	22,800	All retirement programs assumed mutually exclusive, but all Medicare recipients assumed to participate in a retirement program.
Military	7,233	1,000	
Social Security	52,364	20,500	
Railroad	2,250	500	

TABLE 2 (continued)

CONSTRUCTION OF THE 12 PROGRAM CATEGORIES

(Expenditures in millions, Participants in thousands)

PROGRAM	EXPENDITURE	PARTICIPANTS	COMMENTS
Civil Service	6,370	800	
Medicare	21,944	22,800	
J. SSI+Medicaid	9,240	4,706	Mutually inclusive.
SSI	7,585		
Medicaid	1,665		
K. Unemployment Insurance	18,063	12,000	All programs assumed mutually exclusive.
UI	13,490	10,400	
Manpower	1,414	1,000	
Public Service Employment	3,159	600	
L. Residual	57,219	212,303	

Source: W. Lawrence and S. Leeds, An Inventory of Federal Income Transfer Programs: Fiscal Year 1977.

TABLE 3

INPUT DATA FOR SUBSTITUTION ANALYSIS BENCHMARK DEFINITION OF BENEFITS

[1] 1ᴬ: CHILD-POOR (AFDC+MEDICAID)
TOTAL POPULATION = 8,637,000

PROGRAM	AVERAGE BENEFIT	MARGINAL PROBABILITY
A: Food Stamps	$ 240	95.8
B: School Lunch	150	100.0
C: Veterans		
D: Survivors	1,900	3.5
E: Disability		
F: BEOGs		
G: AFDC + Medicaid	784	100.0
H: Medicaid Residual		
I: Retirement		
J: SSI + Medicaid		
K: Unemployment		
L: Residual	105	100.0

[2] 1ᴮ: CHILD-POOR (MEDICAID RESIDUAL)
TOTAL POPULATION = 1,539,000

PROGRAM	AVERAGE BENEFIT	MARGINAL PROBABILITY
A: Food Stamps	$ 240	95.8
B: School Lunch	150	100.0
C: Veterans		
D: Survivors	1,900	3.5
E: Disability		
F: BEOGs		
G: AFDC + Medicaid		
H: Medicaid Residual	152	100.0
I: Retirement		
J: SSI + Medicaid		
K: Unemployment		
L: Residual	105	100.0

[3] 2ᴬ: ADULT-POOR (AFDC+MEDICAID)
TOTAL POPULATION = 4,094,000

PROGRAM	AVERAGE BENEFIT	MARGINAL PROBABILITY
A: Food Stamps	$ 240	55.5
B: School Lunch		
C: Veterans	2,032	6.0
D: Survivors	2,400	2.4
E: Disability	2,775	4.4
F: BEOGs	730	18.5
G: AFDC + Medicaid	1,057	100.0
H: Medicaid Residual		
I: Retirement		
J: SSI + Medicaid		
K: Unemployment		
L: Residual	105	100.0

[4] 2ᴮ: ADULT-POOR (MEDICAID RESIDUAL)
TOTAL POPULATION = 1,108,000

PROGRAM	AVERAGE BENEFIT	MARGINAL PROBABILITY
A: Food Stamps	$ 220	55.5
B: School Lunch		
C: Veterans	2,032	6.0
D: Survivors	2,400	2.4
E: Disability	2,775	4.4
F: BEOGs	730	18.5
G: AFDC + Medicaid		
H: Medicaid Residual	629	100.0
I: Retirement		
J: SSI + Medicaid		
K: Unemployment		
L: Residual	105	100.0

[5] 2ᶜ: ADULT-POOR (SSI+MEDICAID)
TOTAL POPULATION = 2,146,000

A: Food Stamps	$ 240	55.5
B: School Lunch		
C: Veterans	2,032	6.0
D: Survivors	2,400	2.4
E: Disability	2,775	4.4
F: BEOGs	730	18.5
G: AFDC + Medicaid		
H: Medicaid Residual		
I: Retirement		
J: SSI + Medicaid	2,548	100.0
K: Unemployment		
L: Residual	105	100.0

[6] 2ᴰ: ADULT-POOR (UNEMPLOYMENT)
TOTAL POPULATION = 3,454,000

PROGRAM	AVERAGE BENEFIT	MARGINAL PROBABILITY
A: Food Stamps	$ 240	55.5
B: School Lunch		
C: Veterans	2,032	6.0
D: Survivors	2,400	2.4
E: Disability	2,775	4.4
F: BEOGs	730	18.5
G: AFDC + Medicaid		
H: Medicaid Residual		
I: Retirement		
J: SSI + Medicaid		
K: Unemployment	2,184	100.0
L: Residual	105	100.0

[7] 3ᴬ: ELDERLY-POOR (MEDICAID RESIDUAL)
TOTAL POPULATION = 1,300,000

A: Food Stamps	$ 300	48.0
B: School Lunch		
C: Veterans		
D: Survivors	2,400	18.8
E: Disability		
F: BEOGs		
G: AFDC + Medicaid		
H: Medicaid Residual	788	100.0
I: Retirement	3,940	81.9
J: SSI + Medicaid		
K: Unemployment		
L: Residual	105	100.0

[8] 3^B: ELDERLY-POOR (SSI+MEDICAID)
TOTAL POPULATION = 2,595,000

PROGRAM	AVERAGE BENEFIT	MARGINAL PROBABILITY
A: Food Stamps	$ 300	48.0
B: School Lunch		
C: Veterans		
D: Survivors	2,400	18.8
E: Disability		
F: BEOGs		
G: AFDC + Medicaid		
H: Medicaid Residual		
I: Retirement	3,940	81.9
J: SSI + Medicaid	1,555	100.0
K: Unemployment		
L: Residual	105	100.0

[9] 4: CHILD-NONPOOR
TOTAL POPULATION = 53,592,000

A: Food Stamps	$ 80	12.2
B: School Lunch	28	28.0
C: Veterans		
D: Survivors	1,900	4.2
E: Disability		
F: BEOGs		
G: AFDC + Medicaid		
H: Medicaid Residual		
I: Retirement		
J: SSI + Medicaid		
K: Unemployment		
L: Residual	292	100.0

[10] 5: ADULT-NONPOOR
TOTAL POPULATION = 109,966,000

PROGRAM	AVERAGE BENEFIT	MARGINAL PROBABILITY
A: Food Stamps	$ 80	3.6
B: School Lunch		
C: Veterans	2,032	5.3
D: Survivors	2,400	2.1
E: Disability	2,775	3.2
F: BEOGs		
G: AFDC + Medicaid		
H: Medicaid Residual	559	0.6
I: Retirement		
J: SSI + Medicaid		
K: Unemployment	1,297	7.4
L: Residual	292	100.0

[11] 6: ELDERLY-NONPOOR
TOTAL POPULATION = 23,770,000

A: Food Stamps	$ 100	5.0
B: School Lunch		
C: Veterans		
D: Survivors	2,400	18.8
E: Disability		
F: BEOGs		
G: AFDC + Medicaid		
H: Medicaid Residual	892	2.4
I: Retirement	3,940	82.5
J: SSI + Medicaid		
K: Unemployment		
L: Residual	292	100.0

TABLE 4

NOTES ON THE REGROUPING

1. The following program aggregates are retained from the
benchmark definition:
   A. Food Stamps
   B. AFDC+Medicaid
   C. Medicaid residual
   D. SSI+Medicaid
   E. School Lunch
   F. BEOGs
   G. Residual
Expenditure and participation figures are as given in Table 2.

2. In addition, two of our benchmark program aggregates are
retained as optional programs:
   H. Veterans
   I. Unemployment Insurance.
Again, expenditure and participation data are as in Table 2.
These optional programs are not incorporated in the results
presented in this paper.

3. Two new program aggregates are created:
   J. Social Security
   K. Manpower
The assumptions underlying these new aggregates are as follows:

Social Security:
   Social Security = Survivors payments + Disability payments + Retirement payments (including Medicare) 1)
   Survivors—$18,888 million/year is spread over 7.5 mil-
   lion individuals. 50% of the beneficiaries are elderly,
   25% are adults, 25% are children (*Social Security Bulletin,*
   6/78, p. 77 and 2/78, p. 1). Elderly and adult receive
   1.25 × average child benefit (same source). Program is
   not means tested. 2) Disability—$11,625 million/year
   spread over 4.5 million recipients. ⅔ goes to adults, ⅓

TABLE 4 (continued)

goes to children. Program is not means tested. 3) Retirement—$52,364 million in retirement benefits + $21,-944 million in Medicare payments gives a total of $74,-308 million to be spread over 20.5 million elderly. Program is not means tested.

Manpower:

CETA — Manpower & Training Services—$1,414 million/year spread across one million individuals — Public Service Employment—$3,159 million/year spread across 600,000 individuals

All benefits go to poor adults and the two programs are mutually exclusive. Assume benefits go only to those in the adult-poor-residual cell (see below).

4. One new cell redefinition is made. In the basic model among the adult-poor there are four cells, one of which is the "UI cell" (cell 2D). Since that program has been made optional by the regrouping, that cell is reclassified as adult-poor-residual.

TABLE 5

NOTES ON THE ADDITION OF STATE AND LOCAL EXPENDITURES ON FEDERALLY MANDATED PROGRAMS TO THE REGROUPED PROGRAM BASE

1. Unemployment insurance benefits are increased to $1,490/year.

2. The AFDC+Medicaid benefit is increased by $479/year for both children and adults as a result of state expenditures on AFDC.

3. The SSI+Medicaid benefit is increased by $396/year for the adult-poor and by $251/year for the elderly-poor as a result of state/local SSI expenditures.

4. State and local expenditures on Medicaid total $7.9 billion/year. This expenditure is allocated across nine cells as follows:

   $2.1 billion/year goes to AFDC+Medicaid cells
   $3.5 billion/year goes to SSI+Medicaid cells
   $2.3 billion/year goes to Medicaid residual cells

Within AFDC+Medicaid adult-poor benefits are increased by $251/year and child-poor benefits are increased by $124/year. Within SSI+Medicaid benefits are increased by $738/year in both the adult-poor and elderly-poor cells. Within Medicaid residual benefits are increased by $133/year for the child-poor, by $555/year for the adult-poor, by $696/year for the elderly-poor, by $492/year for the adult-nonpoor, and by $785/year for the elderly-nonpoor.

These calculations are based on W. Lawrence and S. Leeds, An Inventory of State and Local Income Transfer Programs: Fiscal Year 1977, *and on articles in the* Social Security Bulletin.

TABLE 6

INPUT DATA FOR SUBSTITUTION ANALYSIS— "REGROUPING"

[1] 1^A: CHILD-POOR (AFDC+MEDICAID)
TOTAL POPULATION = 8,637,000

PROGRAM	AVERAGE BENEFIT	MARGINAL PROBABILITY
A: Food Stamps	$ 240	95.8
B: School Lunch	150	100.0
C: BEOGs		
D: AFDC + Medicaid	784	100.0
E: Medicaid Residual		
F: SSI + Medicaid		
G: Social Security	1,947	5.3
H: Manpower		
I: Tax Expenditure		
J: Residual	105	100.0
K: Veterans		
L: UI		

[2] 1^{B}: Child-Poor (Medicaid Residual)
Total Population = 1,539,000

PROGRAM	AVERAGE BENEFIT	MARGINAL PROBABILITY
A: Food Stamps	$ 240	95.8
B: School Lunch	150	100.0
C: BEOGs		
D: AFDC + Medicaid		
E: Medicaid Residual	152	100.0
F: SSI + Medicaid		
G: Social Security	1,947	5.3
H: Manpower		
I: Tax Expenditure		
J: Residual	105	100.0
K: Veterans		
L: UI		

[3] 2^{A}: Adult-Poor (AFDC+Medicaid)
Total Population = 4,094,000

A: Food Stamps	$ 240	55.5
B: School Lunch		
C: BEOGs	730	18.5
D: AFDC + Medicaid	1,057	100.0
E: Medicaid Residual		
F: SSI + Medicaid		
G: Social Security	2,281	4.0
H: Manpower		
I: Tax Expenditure		
J: Residual	105	100.0
K: Veterans	2,032	6.0
L: UI		

[4] 2ᴮ: ADULT-POOR (MEDICAID RESIDUAL)
TOTAL POPULATION = 1,108,000

PROGRAM	AVERAGE BENEFIT	MARGINAL PROBABILITY
A: Food Stamps	$ 240	55.5
B: School Lunch		
C: BEOGs	730	18.5
D: AFDC + Medicaid		
E: Medicaid Residual	629	100.0
F: SSI + Medicaid		
G: Social Security	2,281	4.0
H: Manpower		
I: Tax Expenditure		
J: Residual	105	100.0
K: Veterans	2,032	6.0
L: UI		

[5] 2ᶜ: ADULT-POOR (SSI+MEDICAID)
TOTAL POPULATION = 2,146,000

A: Food Stamps	$ 240	55.5
B: School Lunch		
C: BEOGs	730	18.5
D: AFDC + Medicaid		
E: Medicaid Residual		
F: SSI + Medicaid	2,548	100.0
G: Social Security	2,281	4.0
H: Manpower		
I: Tax Expenditure		
J: Residual	105	100.0
K: Veterans	2,032	6.0
L: UI		

[6] 2^D: ADULT-POOR (RESIDUAL)
TOTAL POPULATION = 3,459,000

PROGRAM	AVERAGE BENEFIT	MARGINAL PROBABILITY
A: Food Stamps	$ 240	55.5
B: School Lunch		
C: BEOGs	730	18.5
D: AFDC + Medicaid		
E: Medicaid Residual		
F: SSI + Medicaid		
G: Social Security	2,182	4.0
H: Manpower	2,858	46.3
I: Tax Expenditure		
J: Residual	105	100.0
K: Veterans	2,032	6.0
L: UI	1,297	66.2

[7] 3^A: ELDERLY-POOR (MEDICAID RESIDUAL)
TOTAL POPULATION = 1,300,000

A: Food Stamps	$ 300	48.0
B: School Lunch		
C: BEOGs		
D: AFDC + Medicaid		
E: Medicaid Residual	788	100.0
F: SSI + Medicaid		
G: Social Security	3,343	87.8
H: Manpower		
I: Tax Expenditure		
J: Residual	105	100.0
K: Veterans		
L: UI		

[8] 3ᴮ: ELDERLY-POOR (SSI+MEDICAID)
TOTAL POPULATION = 2,595,000

PROGRAM	AVERAGE BENEFIT	MARGINAL PROBABILITY
A: Food Stamps	$ 300	48.0
B: School Lunch		
C: BEOGs		
D: AFDC + Medicaid		
E: Medicaid Residual		
F: SSI + Medicaid	1,555	100.0
G: Social Security	3,343	87.8
H: Manpower		
I: Tax Expenditure		
J: Residual	105	100.0
K: Veterans		
L: UI		

[9] 4: CHII D-NONPOOR
POPULATION = 53,592,000

A: Food Stamps	$ 80	12.2
B: School Lunch	28	28.0
C: BEOGs		
D: AFDC + Medicaid		
E: Medicaid Residual		
F: SSI + Medicaid		
G: Social Security	1,947	5.3
H: Manpower		
I: Tax Expenditure	187	100.0
J: Residual	105	100.0
K: Veterans		
L: UI		

[10] 5: ADULT-NONPOOR
TOTAL POPULATION = 109,966,000

PROGRAM	AVERAGE BENEFIT	MARGINAL PROBABILITY
A: Food Stamps	$ 80	3.6
B: School Lunch		
C: BEOGs		
D: AFDC + Medicaid		
E: Medicaid Residual	559	0.6
F: SSI + Medicaid		
G: Social Security	2,287	4.0
H: Manpower		
I: Tax Expenditure	187	100.0
J: Residual	105	100.0
K: Veterans	2,032	5.3
L: UI	1,297	7.4

[11] 6: ELDERLY-NONPOOR
TOTAL POPULATION = 23,770,000

PROGRAM	AVERAGE BENEFIT	MARGINAL PROBABILITY
A: Food Stamps	$ 100	5.0
B: School Lunch		
C: BEOGs		
D: AFDC + Medicaid		
E: Medicaid Residual	892	2.4
F: SSI + Medicaid		
G: Social Security	3,343	87.8
H: Manpower		
I: Tax Expenditure	187	100.0
J: Residual	105	100.0
K: Veterans		
L: UI		

TABLE 7

INPUT DATA FOR SUBSTITUTION ANALYSIS— REGROUPING + STATE AND LOCAL

[1] 1ᴬ: CHILD-POOR (AFDC+MEDICAID)
TOTAL POPULATION = 8,637,000

PROGRAM	AVERAGE BENEFIT	MARGINAL PROBABILITY
A: Food Stamps	$ 240	95.8
B: School Lunch	150	100.0
C: BEOGs		
D: AFDC + Medicaid	1,387	100.0
E: Medicaid Residual		
F: SSI + Medicaid		
G: Social Security	1,947	5.3
H: Manpower		
I: Tax Expenditure		
J: Residual	105	100.0
K: Veterans		
L: UI		

[2] 1ᴮ: CHILD-POOR (MEDICAID RESIDUAL)

TOTAL POPULATION = 1,539,000

PROGRAM	AVERAGE BENEFIT	MARGINAL PROBABILITY
A: Food Stamps	$ 240	95.8
B: School Lunch	150	100.0
C: BEOGs		
D: AFDC + Medicaid		
E: Medicaid Residual	288	100.0
F: SSI + Medicaid		
G: Social Security	1,947	5.3
H: Manpower		
I: Tax Expenditure		
J: Residual	105	100.0
K: Veterans		
L: UI		

[3] 2ᴬ: ADULT-POOR (AFDC+MEDICAID)

TOTAL POPULATION = 4,094,000

A: Food Stamps	$ 240	55.5
B: School Lunch		
C: BEOGs	730	18.5
D: AFDC + Medicaid	1,787	100.0
E: Medicaid Residual		
F: SSI + Medicaid		
G: Social Security	2,281	4.0
H: Manpower		
I: Tax Expenditure		
J: Residual	105	100.0
K: Veterans	2,032	6.0
L: UI		

[4] 2ᴮ: ADULT-POOR (MEDICAID RESIDUAL)
TOTAL POPULATION = 1,108,000

PROGRAM	AVERAGE BENEFIT	MARGINAL PROBABILITY
A: Food Stamps	$ 240	55.5
B: School Lunch		
C: BEOGs	730	18.5
D: AFDC + Medicaid		
E: Medicaid Residual	1,184	100.0
F: SSI + Medicaid		
G: Social Security	2,281	4.0
H: Manpower		
I: Tax Expenditure		
J: Residual	105	100.0
K: Veterans	2,032	6.0
L: UI		

[5] 2ᶜ: ADULT-POOR (SSI+MEDICAID)
TOTAL POPULATION = 2,146,000

A: Food Stamps	$ 240	55.5
B: School Lunch		
C: BEOGs	730	18.5
D: AFDC + Medicaid		
E: Medicaid Residual		
F: SSI + Medicaid	3,682	100.0
G: Social Security	2,281	4.0
H: Manpower		
I: Tax Expenditure		
J: Residual	105	100.0
K: Veterans	2,032	6.0
L: UI		

[6] 2ᴰ: ADULT-POOR (RESIDUAL)
TOTAL POPULATION = 3,459,000

PROGRAM	AVERAGE BENEFIT	MARGINAL PROBABILITY
A: Food Stamps	$ 240	55.5
B: School Lunch		
C: BEOGs	730	18.5
D: AFDC + Medicaid		
E: Medicaid Residual		
F: SSI + Medicaid		
G: Social Security	2,182	4.0
H: Manpower	2,858	46.3
I: Tax Expenditure		
J: Residual	105	100.0
K: Veterans	2,032	6.0
L: UI	1,490	66.2

[7] 3ᴬ: ELDERLY-POOR (MEDICAID RESIDUAL)
TOTAL POPULATION = 1,300,000

A: Food Stamps	$ 300	48.0
B: School Lunch		
C: BEOGs		
D: AFDC + Medicaid		
E: Medicaid Residual	1,484	100.0
F: SSI + Medicaid		
G: Social Security	3,343	87.8
H: Manpower		
I: Tax Expenditure		
J: Residual	105	100.0
K: Veterans		
L: UI		

[8] 3^B: ELDERLY-POOR (SSI+MEDICAID)
TOTAL POPULATION = 2,595,000

PROGRAM	AVERAGE BENEFIT	MARGINAL PROBABILITY
A: Food Stamps	$ 300	48.0
B: School Lunch		
C: BEOGs		
D: AFDC + Medicaid		
E: Medicaid Residual		
F: SSI + Medicaid	2,544	100.0
G: Social Security	3,343	87.8
H: Manpower		
I: Tax Expenditure		
J: Residual	105	100.0
K: Veterans		
L: UI		

[9] 4: CHILD-NONPOOR
TOTAL POPULATION = 53,592,000

A: Food Stamps	$ 80	12.2
B: School Lunch	28	28.0
C: BEOGs		
D: AFDC + Medicaid		
E: Medicaid Residual		
F: SSI + Medicaid		
G: Social Security	1,947	5.3
H: Manpower		
I: Tax Expenditure	187	100.0
J: Residual	105	100.0
K: Veterans		
L: UI		

[10] 5: ADULT-NONPOOR
TOTAL POPULATION = 109,966,000

PROGRAM	AVERAGE BENEFIT	MARGINAL PROBABILITY
A: Food Stamps	$ 80	3.6
B: School Lunch		
C: BEOGs		
D: AFDC + Medicaid		
E: Medicaid Residual	1,051	0.6
F: SSI + Medicaid		
G: Social Security	2,287	4.0
H: Manpower		
I: Tax Expenditure	187	100.0
J: Residual	105	100.0
K: Veterans	2,032	5.3
L: UI	1,490	7.4

[11] 6: ELDERLY-NONPOOR
TOTAL POPULATION = 23,770,000

PROGRAM	AVERAGE BENEFIT	MARGINAL PROBABILITY
A: Food Stamps	$ 100	5.0
B: School Lunch		
C: BEOGs		
D: AFDC + Medicaid		
E: Medicaid Residual	1,677	2.4
F: SSI + Medicaid		
G: Social Security	3,343	87.8
H: Manpower		
I: Tax Expenditure	187	100.0
J: Residual	105	100.0
K: Veterans		
L: UI		

TABLE 8

CUMULATIVE DISTRIBUTION FUNCTION OF BENEFITS USING ALTERNATIVE DEFINITIONS OF BENEFITS

% OF POPULATION RECEIVING
BENEFIT LEVEL OR LESS

BENEFIT LEVEL	1	2	3
$ 300	59.8%	66.2%	60.1%
400	68.4	75.5	68.9
500	69.1	75.7	68.9
600	69.3	76.2	69.1
700	69.3	76.2	69.5
800	69.6	76.4	69.8
900	69.8	76.9	69.8
1,000	70.1	77.1	69.8
1,100	71.0	77.5	69.8
1,200	71.9	78.1	69.8
1,300	74.7	81.7	69.9
1,400	75.5	82.5	70.3
1,500	76.4	82.5	70.3
1,600	78.8	82.5	70.4
1,700	78.8	82.8	72.7
1,800	79.0	82.8	74.1
1,900	79.2	83.0	78.8
2,000	79.2	83.0	78.8
2,100	79.2	83.0	79.2
2,200	80.2	83.6	80.3
2,300	81.1	84.4	80.9
2,400	83.5	84.4	83.5

Notes: Definition 1—Benchmark Definition, cf. Tables 2 and 3
Definition 2—Regrouping, optional programs *excluded*, cf. Tables 4 and 6
Definition 3—Regrouping, optional programs *included*, plus state and local expenditures on federally mandated programs, cf. Tables 5 and 7.

All figures are derived via linear interpolation.

TABLE 9

GROSS CASHOUT RATIOS
USING ALTERNATIVE DEFINITIONS
OF BENEFITS

DEMOGRANT	1	2	3
$ 300	119.9	119.3	119.6
400	104.3	102.2	104.0
500	96.3	93.4	94.6
600	88.6	85.0	87.8
700	82.7	78.5	83.1
800	79.1	74.4	78.7
900	76.1	71.2	76.1
1,000	73.8	68.7	73.9
1,100	72.0	66.6	71.8
1,200	70.4	64.9	70.4
1,300	69.0	63.4	69.1
1,400	67.6	61.8	68.0
1,500	66.4	60.6	67.1
1,600	65.3	59.5	66.3
1,700	64.2	58.3	65.5
1,800	63.3	57.5	64.9
1,900	62.3	56.7	64.1
2,000	61.6	56.0	63.3
2,100	60.9	55.4	62.5
2,200	60.2	54.8	61.8
2,300	59.6	54.3	61.1
2,400	59.0	53.8	60.3

See the notes to Table 8.

TABLE 10

PER CAPITA EXCESS BURDENS
USING ALTERNATIVE
DEFINITIONS OF BENEFITS

DEMOGRANT	1	2	3
$ 300	$ −59.7	$ −57.7	$ −58.6
400	−17.4	−8.8	−15.9
500	29.0	44.7	31.1
600	75.4	98.1	77.9
700	122.0	151.8	124.4
800	168.7	205.6	171.1
900	215.5	259.5	217.8
1,000	262.2	313.4	264.3
1,100	308.9	367.4	310.6
1,200	355.6	421.5	356.6
1,300	403.3	467.5	402.6
1,400	453.7	534.2	448.7
1,500	504.6	592.4	494.6
1,600	555.6	650.4	540.4
1,700	609.4	708.3	586.2
1,800	662.9	765.7	632.6
1,900	716.3	823.1	682.3
2,000	769.5	880.4	735.6
2,100	822.5	937.4	788.7
2,200	875.6	994.3	842.0
2,300	929.5	1,051.8	896.0
2,400	985.2	1,109.5	952.3

See the notes to Table 8.

FIGURE 1

CUMULATIVE DISTRIBUTION
FUNCTION OF BENEFITS

Percentage of Population
Receiving Benefit Level or Less

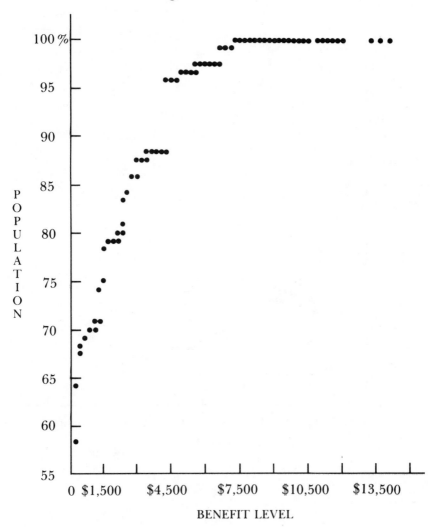

FIGURE 2

CASHOUT RATIO
BY DEMOGRANT LEVEL

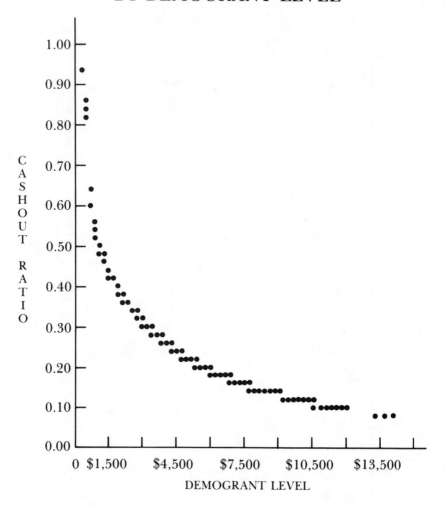

FIGURE 3

GROSS CASHOUT RATIO
BY DEMOGRANT LEVEL

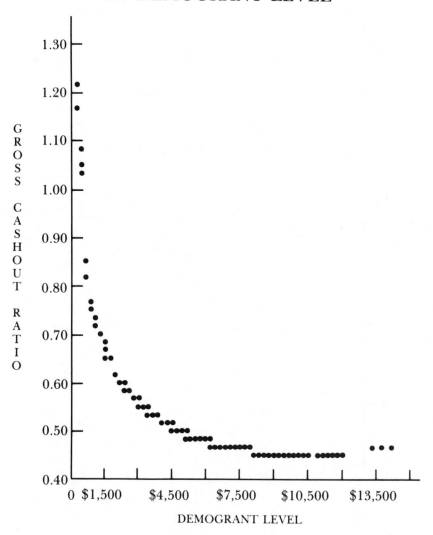

FIGURE 4

PER CAPITA EXCESS BURDEN
BY DEMOGRANT LEVEL

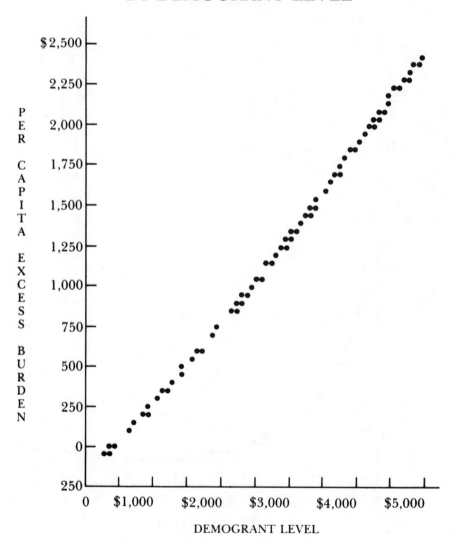

DEMOGRANT LEVEL

Index

ACTION, 77
AFDC, *see* Aid to Families with Dependent Children
AFL-CIO, 86
aging, programs for, 27, 38. *See also* Medicare
agriculture
    corporate, 30
    Department of,
        food stamps, 28, 109, 112–13, 132–33
        price supports, 24–25
Aid to Families with Dependent Children (AFDC)
    in Carter administration, 87
    consolidate with food stamps, 113, 132
    differentials among states, 39
    eligibility for, 27, 32, 79
    energy aid for, 91–92
    major element of welfare, 25, 27, 33, 36, 37
    promotes family breakup, 32, 45–52, 115
    in substitution analysis, 141, 145
    "tax" rate for, 44, 115
Alaska, 26–27
alien workers, 57–58, 121
annuities, 54

benefit reduction rate, 42–44
    in AFDC, 115
    in FAP, 83
    in Social Security, 58
Blacks, 15–16
blind, 61–62

block grant system, 91–92
Braybrooke, David, 128–129
Brookings Institution, 107
budget, federal, 26, 39, 57, 80, 95
Bureau of Labor Statistics, 92

California, 1972 presidential primary, 85
Carey, Hugh L., 43
Carter, Jimmy, 19, 60–61, 87–88, 125, 128
cashout, 137–39, 146–54
categorical aid, 31–40, 95, 108. *See also* eligibility; entitlements
CETA, *see* Comprehensive Employment and Training Act,
Chamber of Commerce of the U.S., Council on Trends and Perspectives, 86
child care, 33
child support laws, 51
children's allowances, 46, 82–83
cities, 16, 77–78, 131
Commission on Income Maintenance Programs (Heineman Commission), 82, 117
Community Action Program (CAP), 74, 76, 79
Community Services Administration (CSA), 76
Comprehensive Employment and Training Act (CETA), 37, 93–94
Congress
    Earned Income Tax Credit, 50
    energy aid, 91–93
    FAP, 83–84

Congress (*continued*)
  mandatory retirement, 57, 69
  politics in, 109–10, 124
  power of, 39, 80, 108
  PBJI, 87–88
  tax relief for the elderly, 27
  welfare reform, 19
  windfall-profits tax, 90–91
Conte, Silvio O., 93
crop subsidies, 24–25, 30

Danziger, Sheldon, 78
Defense, Department of, 28
demogrant, 137–40, 146–54. *See also*
  Graduated Income Supplement
dependency system, 18–20, 58, 61, 65,
  71–72, 79, 81, 88, 106, 110–11,
  122, 133, 138
Depression, The Great, 18, 56, 72
disability benefits, 32, 36, 39, 59–62,
  71, 91–92, 132, 145
disincentives, work, 16, 19, 34, 41–44,
  95, 121
  in AFDC, 113
  in FAP, 83
  in Social Security, 53–62, 71, 81
  in unemployment insurance, 63–69
Douglas, Paul H., 54

Earned Income Tax Credit, 37, 50
economic system, *see* dependency system; free enterprise system
education programs, 25, 37
Eisenhower, Dwight D., 72
elderly
  discrimination against, 57
  incomes of, 58
  see also aging, programs for; mandatory retirement; Social Security
eligibility, 31–40
  AFDC, 47
  disability, 61–62
  Medicaid, 50–51
  multiple, 108
  unemployment, 65
  universal, 115–16
Emergency Assistance, 37
energy aid, 89–95
Energy, Department of, 93–94
entitlements, 39. *See also* eligibility

Fair Share, 84–86
Family Assistance Plan (FAP), 82–88

family policy, 45–52, 111
farm programs, *see* agriculture; crop
  subsidies; price supports
Feldstein, Martin, 66
Finch, Robert, 84
Food Stamps, 26, 28, 35–37, 49, 74,
  109, 112–13, 131–33, 141–42
Ford, Gerald R., 19, 86
Foster Grandparents, 75, 77
fraud
  in OEO CAP programs, 76
  in unemployment insurance, 67–
  68
  in welfare system, 32, 37, 38, 49, 60,
  123
free enterprise system, 17–20, 58, 68,
  88
  integrating welfare recipients, 119,
  122, 133–34
Friedman, Milton, 82

General Accounting Office (GAO),
  65–66
Graduated Income Supplement,
  effect of, 111–23
  cost and operation of, 125–27,
  131–34
Great Society, 81
Green Thumb, 75
Griffiths, Martha, 87
Gutmann, Peter M., 67–68

Hawaii,
  AFDC payments in, 39
  energy aid for, 93
Head Start, 38, 75, 77, 79
Health and Human Services, Department of, 93, 109, 133
Health, Education and Welfare, Department of, 28, 52, 77, 84, 86
health services, 26, 38. *See also* Medicaid; Medicare
Heineman, Ben, 82
Housing and Urban Development, Department of, 16
housing, subsidized, 16, 25, 33, 35, 37,
  92, 113
Humphrey, Hubert H., 85, 87
Humphrey-Hawkins "full employment" bill, 87

IBM, 70
incentives, work, 17, 19

in Carter proposals, 60–61
in FAP, 83–84
in GIS, 112, 115, 119, 133
in income supplements, 117
in NIT, 82
in tax rates, 119
in welfare reform, 111
in welfare system, 114
Income Security Plan, 86
income support programs, 23–30, 96–
    105
definition of, 125, 144
economic impact of, 78, 80
managed through IRS, 119
manipulation of, 60
replacement with GIS, 125–27
state programs, 29
see also AFDC; categorical aid; en-
    ergy aid; Food Stamps; Social
    Security; unemployment insur-
    ance
income tax, 16, 58. See also Internal
    Revenue Service
income transfer programs, see income
    support programs
Indiana, Medicaid eligibility in, 51
Indians, American,
health care for, 26
credit program, 27
OEO programs, 75
in-kind assistance, 25–26, 113–14, 144.
    See also specific program titles
Institute for Research on Poverty, 78
Institute for Socioeconomic Studies,
    The, 11, 12, 24, 38, 87, 96, 126–
    27, 131, 137
The Journal, 87
insurance, 25, 27, 35. See also specific
    program titles
Internal Revenue Service
Internal Revenue Code, 26, 47
managing income support pro-
    grams, 28, 111, 119–21
Inventory of Federal Income Transfer Pro-
    grams–Fiscal Year 1977, 24, 26,
    96, 114, 144
Inventory of State and Local Income Trans-
    fer Programs–Fiscal Year 1977, 38–
    39, 96

Jefferson, Thomas, 17
Job Corps, 74, 77, 79
jobs programs, 78

Johnson, Lyndon B., 57, 73–80, 82, 88,
    110

Kennedy, Edward M., 45
Kennedy, John F., 73, 74, 82

Labor, Department of, 77. See also Bu-
    reau of Labor Statistics
legal services for the poor, 75
Lindblom, Charles E., 128
Long, Russell, B., 83–84
Louisiana, energy aid for, 93

McGovern, George, 84–86
Maine, energy aid for, 93
Manciewicz, Frank, 85
mandatory retirement, 57, 69–71
Manpower Development and Train-
    ing, 74
marginal tax rate
effect of demogrant on, 137, 139
in FAP, 83
in NIT, 82
uniform, 119
MATCH, 140
Meany, George, 86
Medicaid, 31, 33–34, 37, 49–51, 89
cause of high cost of medical care,
    114
definition of, 36
in substitution analysis, 145
Medicare, 25, 36, 60, 142
Michigan Income Dynamics, 140
migrant workers, 75
migration, see welfare migration
military retirement program, 28
minorities, see Alaska; alien workers;
    Blacks; Indians, American; mi-
    grant workers
Mississippi, AFDC payments in, 39
Moynihan, Daniel Patrick, 82

National Association of Social Workers
    (NASW), 83
National Journal, 76
National Welfare Rights Organization,
    83
negative income tax (NIT), 82, 117,
    119
Neighborhood Youth Corps, 74, 77
New Deal, 42, 88
New Hampshire, energy aid for, 93
New York City

New York City (*continued*)
Rand Corp. study, 32
New York State
  Apple farmers import labor, 121
  employment service, 15
  energy aid programs, 93–94
  Medicaid eligibility in, 51
New York Times, 68–69, 83
Nixon, Richard M., 19, 76, 82–86
nursing homes, 51–52
nutritional assistance, 26, 28, 38. *See also* Food Stamps; School breakfast/lunch program

Office of Economic Opportunity (OEO), 74–77, 82

Palmer, John L., 107
Peace Corps, 74, 77
pensions, 26, 56, 58, 70–71
Plotnik, Robert, 78
poverty, *see* "War on Poverty"
price supports, 24, 25, 30. *See also* crop subsidies
productivity, 17–19, 69–71, 122–23
Program for Better Jobs and Income (PBJI), 87–88
Pruitt-Igoe housing project, 113
public assistance, *see* welfare system
Public Utilities Regulatory Policies Act (PURPA), 94

Rand Corporation, 32
"relief," *see* welfare system
retirement
  benefits, 54–59
  mandatory, *see* mandatory retirement
  military program, 28
Richardson, Elliot, 84
Roosevelt, Franklin D., 18, 42, 72, 80

Safe Flight Instrument Corporation, 15, 70
St. Louis, 113
school breakfast/lunch program, 33, 36
seasonal workers, 66
Shriver, R. Sargent, 74, 82
Social Security
  Act of 1935, 54, 58, 64, 81, 129
  Advisory Council, 61

benefits, *see* disability; retirement; survivors
  contributions from aliens, 57–58
  earnings limitation, 56, 59
  financing of, 57–58
  old age, survivors and disability insurance (OASDI), 35, 55
  payroll tax, 58
  quirks, 34–35
  in substitution analysis, 142, 149
  Supplemental Security Income (SSI), *see* disability benefits
  taxation of, 55, 58, 120
  trust fund, 57
  work disincentives in, 55–57
social workers' union, *see* National Association of Social Workers
Stockman, David A., 49
subsidies, *see* income support programs
substitution concept, 126–127
  research by The Institute for Socioeconomic Studies, 127, 137
  technique, 132, 138–54
subterranean economy, 67, 117
survivors benefits, 31

tax credit, 25, 111, 115
tax policy, 137
tax recoupment, 137–39, 146–54
tax relief, 25–27
Texas, energy aid for, 93

underground economy, *see* subterranean economy
uniform benefits, 111, 118
unemployment, 18–20
  compensation, 35, 65, 66, 68, 80
  insurance, 63–69
  policy, 68
  in substitution/analysis, 145
  trust fund, 35, 64
  work requirement, 67
Upward Bound, 75, 77

veterans
  Administration, 28
  benefits, 28
  health care, 25, 28
  insurance, 27
  pensions, 35, 37
  in substitution analysis, 142
Vietnam War, 57

Volunteers in Service to America
    (VISTA), 74, 77

"War on Poverty", 73–81, 88, 110
waste, 32, 33, 38, 76, 123
Weinberger, Caspar, 86–87
welfare bureaucracy, 110
    causes of, 130
    cost of, 38
    elimination of, 116, 119, 125
    size of, 73, 95, 108
welfare policy, 39, 46, 49, 50, 117
welfare reform, 19, 81–88, 106–23
    comprehensive vs. incremental, 124,
        128–29
    federal administration of, 130
    presidential commission on, 82, 117
    principals of, 111–16, 129–30,
        133–34

welfare system, 17–20
    eliminates incentive, 52, 86
    Humphrey supported, 85
    migration, 77–78, 118–19, 130
    perpetuates poverty, 73, 106
    promotes family breakup, 52
    a trap, 45
    welfare "class", 34
    welfare "tax", 42, 115
    see also fraud; income support pro-
        grams; waste
Wiley, George A., 83–84
windfall-profits tax, 90–91, 95
Wisconsin, University of, 78
work disincentives, see disincentives,
    work
work ethic, 18
work incentives, see incentives, work
Work Incentive Program (WIN), 37